D0190384

THE
HUNGRY
Healthy
STUDENT
COOKBOOK

**MORE THAN 200 RECIPES
THAT ARE DELICIOUS AND
GOOD FOR YOU TOO**

spruce

An Hachette UK Company
www.hachette.co.uk

First published in Great Britain in 2016 by Spruce, a division
of Octopus Publishing Group Ltd, Carmelite House,
50 Victoria Embankment, London EC4Y 0DZ
www.octopusbooks.co.uk
www.octopusbooksusa.com

Copyright © Octopus Publishing Group Ltd 2016

Distributed in the US by Hachette Book Group, 1290 Avenue
of the Americas, 4th and 5th Floors, New York, NY 10020

Distributed in Canada by Canadian Manda Group,
664 Annette St., Toronto, Ontario, Canada M6S 2C8

All rights reserved. No part of this work may be reproduced or utilized
in any form or by any means, electronic or mechanical, including
photocopying, recording, or by any information storage and retrieval
system, without the prior written permission of the publisher.

ISBN 978-1-84601-529-8

Printed and bound in China

10 9 8 7 6 5 4 3

The recipes in this book have been labelled as suitable for Gluten Free,
Vegan, and Vegetarian diets. Vegetarians should look for the 'V' symbol
on a cheese to ensure it is made with vegetarian rennet. There are
vegetarian forms of Parmesan, Feta, Cheddar, Cheshire, Red Leicester,
dolcelatte, and many goats' cheeses, among others.

Standard level spoon measurement are used
in all recipes.
1 tablespoon = one 15 ml spoon
1 teaspoon = one 5 ml spoon

Ovens should be preheated to the specific
temperature – if using a fan-assisted oven,
follow manufacturer's instructions for
adjusting the time and the temperature.

Pepper should be freshly ground black
pepper unless otherwise stated.

SPICED ROAST CHICKEN WITH LIME

Contents

SPINACH & PEA FRITATTA

WEST INDIAN BEEF & BEAN STEW

INTRODUCTION

Leaving home and living on your own for the first time is both challenging and exciting. And while you're settling in, meeting new people, and getting to grips with your independence, food can swiftly slide down the list of priorities. But it's important to establish good habits from the beginning and to try to incorporate healthy eating as part of a healthy lifestyle. It's no more expensive or time consuming to eat healthily as a student; it just takes a little planning. So, if you want to enjoy a varied diet that doesn't have to be emptied onto your plate from a plastic container, it's time to up your game in the kitchen and get to grips with ingredients and cooking techniques.

COOKING FOR YOURSELF

Whether you live on campus or in shared accommodation, you'll need to be organized when it comes to budgeting and shopping for food. If you're moving in with people you already know, it makes sense to work out what kitchen equipment you'll need and divide the list among you. That way, you won't end up with six juicers and an empty cabinet without plates and dishes. Likewise, when it comes to shopping, your budget will stretch much farther if you pool together your resources and shop as a household. You can buy ingredients in bulk and make the most of any discount or coupon deals. However, you will need to take individual preferences and diets into account—it's hardly fair if the vegetarian among you has to fund a weekly meat feast.

FOODIE FRICTION

Food can be the cause of tension in shared student houses, so it's a good idea to set out a few simple rules when you first move in. That doesn't mean installing CCTV in the refrigerator and keeping your favorite cereal in a safe in case anyone tries to dig into a bowl for breakfast. But it does mean working out a cooking and shopping rota if you're planning to eat meals together. You'll need to decide on a feasible weekly food budget and allocate someone to take control of it. Obviously, you won't all be eating at home every night of the week, so you could, for example, plan and enjoy midweek meals together and then let everyone fend for themselves on the weekend.

WHERE TO SHOP

The Internet can make it easier for a shared household to do their food shopping. You can choose a time when everyone is around so you all get to have a say in what makes it into the shopping cart. A meal planner will make it much easier to shop within budget and, if it is agreed in advance, there'll be fewer "discussions" about which ingredients you need to buy. Shopping online means you don't all have to trek to the supermarket together—a particular drag if no one has a car. You can order your shopping for a week and get it delivered when you know someone will be at home.

Local farmers' markets often offer value for money, especially for seasonal produce. They offer a great way to shop for a special weekend meal, or local ingredients that you won't see in the supermarket.

STOCK UP YOUR PANTRY

Your first grocery shop will probably be the most expensive, because you'll need to stock up on pantry essentials that form the basis of many meals. Alternatively, as with equipment, you could devise a list and ask everyone to bring a few items when you move in. Here's the lowdown on what you should line your cupboards with on moving-in day.

- **CONDIMENTS** Salt and black pepper are essential for many recipes and good seasoning will liven up most dishes. You will also need vegetable oil for cooking and olive oil for dressings and sauces. Ketchup, mayonnaise, and mustard are also staples.

- **BUTTER** Toast is a student staple, so a good supply of butter, margarine, or other spread is essential. It is an important ingredient for mashed potatoes.

- **SPICES** You don't need a full range of spices in a student kitchen, but if you stock up on chili powder, turmeric, cumin, and maybe some mustard and fennel seeds, you'll be able to rustle up a half decent casserole. Bouillon cubes and powders are also handy when you don't have any fresh broth made up (see Back to Basics, pages 242-51).

- **ONIONS AND GARLIC** Like salt and pepper, onion and garlic are vital ingredients in all kinds of dishes across all cuisines. These have a long shelf life if you keep them in the refrigerator.

- **PASTA AND RICE** Casseroles, salads, risottos, soups, pilafs ... the list is endless, and a good stock of pasta and rice will see you through the lean times.

- **LEGUMES AND GRAINS** Split peas, lentils, couscous, bulgur wheat and quinoa are wonderful pantry staples for meals in their own right, or used to bulk up soups and stews.

- **CANS** Cans of beans (kidney beans, lima beans, and so on), corn kernels, and chickpeas (garbanzo beans) are reliable favorites when the budget is tight. They are cheap and nutritious and can be swiftly turned into a casserole or chili with a few extra ingredients.

- **FREEZER STAPLES** A lot of student accommodation experience a lack of a decent freezer, and you might have to make do with a couple of shelves or a small compartment at the top of the refrigerator. But as long as there's space for some frozen vegetables and a few containers of leftovers, you should be able to get by.

HEALTHY WEEK MEAL PLANNER

	MONDAY	TUESDAY	WEDNESDAY	THURSDAY	FRIDAY	SATURDAY	SUNDAY
BREAKFAST	MANGO & ORANGE SMOOTHIE (page 12)	BERRY, HONEY & YOGURT CUPS (page 16)	MIXED GRAIN PORRIDGE (page 21)	MAPLE-GLAZED GRANOLA WITH FRUIT (page 20)	APPLE & YOGURT MUESLI (page 19)	CORN & BACON MUFFINS (page 26)	BANANA & RAISIN PANCAKES (page 24)
LUNCH	TURKEY & AVOCADO SALAD (page 165)	FALAFEL PITA POCKETS (page 37)	HEARTY MINESTRONE (page 48)	TANDOORI CHICKEN SALAD (page 164)	TUNA & CORN WRAPS (page 43)	BAKED SWEET POTATOES (page 84)	SPINACH & PEA FRITTATA (page 206)
DINNER	PASTA WITH SPICY LENTILS (page 129)	STEAMED GINGER FISH (page 198)	SMOKED MACKEREL SUPERFOOD SALAD (page 158)	RANCH-STYLE EGGS (page 70)	FAST CHICKEN CURRY (page 190)	FIVE VEGGIE PIZZA (page 211)	SWEDISH MEATBALLS (page 100)

ESSENTIAL EQUIPMENT

If you're starting from scratch, you'll probably have to beg or borrow most of your kitchen equipment, which means you won't be cooking with state-of-the-art pans and processors. But you don't actually need that many gadgets and gizmos to rustle up any of the recipes in this book. With just a few basics, you can eat well and even impress your friends with more daring creations when you develop some culinary confidence. Here's a list of the equipment you'll need to avoid a bread and baked beans diet.

UTENSILS Set of measuring cups and spoons, liquid measuring cup, two mixing bowls in different sizes, wooden spoon, rolling pin, grater, spatula, cutting board, vegetable peeler, whisk, colander, sharp knives (one small for prepping vegetables and fruit and one large for chopping, slicing bread, etc).

POTS AND PANS Large and small saucepans (with lids), large nonstick skillet, steamer (useful, but a metal colander over a saucepan works fine). A wok is also handy for quick stir-fries, but not essential.

COOKWARE Baking sheet, roasting pan, flameproof casserole dish or Dutch oven, large rectangular ovenproof dish (for lasagnes, casseroles, etc), wire cooling rack, cake pans, muffin pans, and pastry cutters (if you're a baker).

A blender or food processor is a luxury item that will prove useful if you find your cooking mojo. But don't worry if you can't get your hands on these pricier pieces of culinary equipment—a relatively inexpensive handheld blender will do the job for most soups and smoothies and your knife skills will be all the better for chopping everything by hand.

GETTING YOUR FRUIT & VEGGIES

The USDA recommends that college-age adults have 2 cups of fruit every day (1 cup of 100 percent fruit juice or 1/2 cup of dried fruit counts as 1 cup of fruit) plus 2 1/2 cups of vegetables daily if you are a female or 3 cups if you are male. It's easy to lose track, especially if you're busy studying and socializing and grabbing food on the go. Here are some quick ways to cram plenty of vitamins and minerals into your diet:

1 Get in the habit of having fruit with breakfast and you're already on your way to 2 cups a day before you leave the house. It could be chopped fruit with muesli or granola, a glass of fresh juice, or a sliced banana on your cornflakes or oatmeal.

2 Steam vegetables to serve as an accompaniment to dinner or have a side salad.

3 Change your usual midmorning bag of potato chips for some chopped carrots and hummus.

4 Try ordering a fruit smoothie instead of that double-shot latte; you'll get the same buzz while upping your daily dose of fruit.

5 Dig into a baked potato or toast piled high with baked beans—these beans count toward your veggie intake, so make this your new favorite—and inexpensive—lunch.

HEALTHY HABITS

It's easy to get into bad habits when you're responsible for all your own food shopping and meal prep. You might have the best intentions about staying healthy and eating a nutritious and balanced diet, but whether you're heading straight from a lecture to the cafeteria, or you're craving a sugar hit to get you through a marathon essay-writing session, it's easy to fall off the well-being wagon and reach for salty snacks, energy drinks, and chocolate bars.

SUGAR RUSH Sugar offers a short-term solution to lethargy but it won't keep you company for long, because the initial buzz is swiftly followed by an energy lapse and a craving for more sugary junk food. It's the added sugars in food and drink that are the real enemy, especially if the food doesn't have any other redeeming nutritional features. Food labeling is becoming more transparent, so always check the label to see just how much sugar the product contains and to give yourself a reality check and a nudge to choose a healthier alternative.

Soft drinks, processed snacks, some breakfast cereals, and pasta sauces are all major culprits, but making simple changes, such as having oatmeal for breakfast, making your own sauce, and cutting out the unnecessary cookies and chocolate bars can all make a big difference. And do you really need two or three spoons of sugar in your morning coffee? Think of added sugar as empty calories—something your body doesn't need and something you can easily train it not to crave.

CALL TIME ON DRINKING A healthy lifestyle doesn't mean you have to treat your body like a temple 24/7. It's all about balance and making sensible choices most of the time. As long as you're aware of what you should be consuming, the odd splurge or treat won't be the end of the world.

The same is true for drinking alcohol, once you are legally old enough, of course. When you enter that stage of your life, it's important to know your limitations and be aware of how much alcohol you're drinking. It can quickly add up, even during the more innocuous evenings in a bar or club. The recommended U.S. government guidelines are that women should have no more than 1 standard drink per day and men 2 standard drinks per day. However, different types of alcoholic beverages have different amounts of alcohol content.

BUDGETING

Boring as it may be, unless you want to spend the last month of each term hiding in your hovel and eating plain rice, budgeting is a necessary part of student life. Each recipe in this book is rated from 1 to 3, with 1s providing end-of-term saviors that can be scraped together for a pittance, and 3s to splash out and impress all your friends.

What's a standard drink?

Different types of alcoholic beverages have varying amounts of alcohol content, so don't base a drink on volume. Below are examples of what is considered one standard drink:

- 12 fl oz regular beer (about 5% alcohol)
- 8-9 fl oz malt liquor (about 7% alcohol)
- 5 fl oz table wine (about 12% alcohol)
- 1½ fl oz shot of 80-proof spirits such as rum, vodka, tequila, whiskey, or gin (about 40% alcohol)

MOOD BOOSTERS

Leaving home for the first time is a major life event, and while it signals a huge leap in your independence, it can have a big impact on your emotional state. It's normal to feel homesick and, as mentioned, it's important to take care of yourself by eating well, exercising, and not overdoing it on unhealthy snacks. As you settle into your studies, you'll be putting a lot of pressure on your brain, which makes it important to boost your body with bundles of vitamin-rich foods. If you're having a bad day, feeling tired, and finding it difficult to concentrate, there are a few foods that can help lift you up and give you a boost. Here are five to get you started:

WATER We should drink at least eight 8 fl oz glasses of fluids every day—even more in hot weather or when exercising—and the more that amount is made up of water, the better. A small drop in the amount of fluids you drink can quickly affect your mood and you'll begin to get dehydrated, have a headache, and feel tired.

DARK CHOCOLATE Yes, it does contain sugar, but dark chocolate also releases endorphins (happy chemicals) in your brain. Of course, everything in moderation, so stick to a couple of squares—just enough to put a smile on your face.

OILY FISH Salmon, sardines, mackerel, and tuna all contain omega-3, which is an important nutrient that can help enhance your mood by calming you down if you feel stressed.

GREEN TEA This should be your hot beverage of choice when you're studying for exams—the thiamine in green tea can help you concentrate.

CARBOHYDRATES These are a vital component of a balanced diet and, if you cut out the carbs, you might not feel your best. Carbs help your brain to produce serotonin, and a regular intake of slow-release, whole-grain carbohydrates will help to keep you focused and full of energy.

Breakfast & Lunch Box

BROWN RICE SALAD WITH
PEANUTS & RAISINS

MAPLE-GLAZED GRANOLA WITH FRUIT

BERRY, HONEY & YOGURT CUPS

BREAKFAST SMOOTHIE Ⓥ

AFFORDABILITY 1

1 Put all the ingredients into a blender or food processor and blend until smooth and creamy.

2 Pour into 2-3 glasses and serve immediately.

1 tablespoon pomegranate juice
1 small ripe banana, peeled and sliced
1¼ cups soy milk
1 tablespoon almonds
1 tablespoon rolled oats
½ teaspoon honey
1½ teaspoons ground flaxseed
2 tablespoons plain yogurt

Serves **2-3**
Prep time **10 minutes**

HEALTHY TIP

WAKE UP AND REHYDRATE Keep a large glass of water by your bed and drink it as soon as you wake up in the morning. This will help your body to rehydrate while you're getting ready for the day.

Banana & Peanut Butter SMOOTHIE Ⓥ

PEANUT BUTTER MAY SEEM LIKE AN UNUSUAL INGREDIENT IN A SMOOTHIE BUT, IN FACT, IT COMBINES WONDERFULLY WELL WITH BANANAS TO MAKE A RICH, SATISFYING DRINK. PEANUTS CONTAIN RESVERATROL, PLANT STEROLS, AND OTHER PHYTOCHEMICALS, WHICH, ACCORDING TO RESEARCH, HAVE CARDIO-PROTECTIVE AND CANCER-INHIBITING PROPERTIES. THIS HIGH-CALCIUM DRINK IS A GREAT PICK-ME-UP AFTER EXERCISE.

1 ripe banana
1¼ cups low-fat milk
1 tablespoon smooth peanut
  butter or 2 teaspoons tahini

Serves **2**
Prep time **10 minutes,
plus freezing**

1 Peel and slice the banana, put it into a freezer-proof container, and freeze for at least 2 hours or overnight.

2 Put the frozen banana, the milk, and peanut butter or tahini into a blender or food processor and blend until smooth.

3 Pour into 2 glasses and serve immediately.

NUTRITIONAL TIP
Tahini is a delicious paste made from crushed sesame seeds. Weight for weight, sesame seeds contain ten times more calcium than milk. This smoothie is an excellent source of vitamins C, B_1, B_2, B_6, and B_{12}, folic acid, niacin, calcium, copper, potassium, zinc, magnesium, and phosphorus.

MANGO & ORANGE SMOOTHIE

Vegan

1 ripe mango, peeled, pitted, and chopped, or 1 cup frozen mango chunks
²/₃ cup plain soy yogurt
²/₃ cup orange juice
finely grated zest and juice of 1 lime
2 teaspoons agave nectar, or to taste

Serves **2**
Prep time **10 minutes**

1 Blend together the mango, yogurt, orange juice, lime zest and juice, and agave nectar in a blender or food processor until smooth.

2 Pour into 2 glasses and serve immediately.

VARIATION
For a ginger banana smoothie, blend together 1 ripe, peeled banana, ³/₄ inch piece of fresh ginger root, peeled and grated, ²/₃ cup plain soy yogurt, and ²/₃ cup orange or mango juice in a blender or food processor until smooth. Sweeten to taste with agave nectar, pour into 2 glasses, and serve immediately.

AFFORDABILITY **1**

AVOCADO & BANANA
SMOOTHIE (V)

1 small ripe avocado
1 small ripe banana
1 cup skim milk

Serves **1**
Prep time **10 minutes**

1 Peel the avocado, remove the pit, and coarsely chop the flesh. Peel and slice the banana.

2 Put the avocado, banana, and milk into a blender or food processor and blend together until smooth.

3 Pour into a glass, add a couple of ice cubes, and serve immediately.

HEALTHY TIP

IN THE TROPICS, avocados are often called poor man's butter, because of their creamy texture and high fat content. Unlike butter, however, most of the fat is monounsaturated—the kind that helps lower levels of "bad" cholesterol (or low-density lipoproteins) while raising levels of "good" cholesterol (or high-density lipoproteins). Just one avocado provides around half the recommended daily intake of vitamin B_6. This smoothie is an excellent source of vitamins C, E, B_1, B_2, B_6, and B_{12}, as well as folic acid, calcium, potassium, copper, zinc, magnesium, and phosphorus.

GINGERED APPLE & CARROT JUICE

Vegan

6 carrots, peeled and cut
  into chunks
3 sweet, crisp apples, cored
  and cut into chunks
1 inch piece of fresh ginger
  root, peeled

1 Feed the carrot and apple chunks through a juicer with the ginger.

2 Pour the juice into 2 glasses and serve immediately.

Serves **2**
Prep time **10 minutes**

AFFORDABILITY 1

HEALTHY TIP

THIS VIBRANT JUICE is packed with carotenoids. These are converted to vitamin A by the body. They are particularly important for normal tissue growth and are an antioxidant.

Watermelon Cooler

Vegan

2/3 cup watermelon cubes
2/3 cup hulled strawberries
1/2 cup water
small handful of mint or tarragon
  leaves, plus extra to serve (optional)

1 Put the watermelon cubes and strawberries into the freezer until frozen solid.

2 Put the frozen melon and strawberries into a blender or food processor, add the water and mint or tarragon, and blend until smooth.

3 Pour the mixture into 2 glasses, decorate with mint or tarragon leaves, if desired, and serve immediately.

Serves **2**
Prep time **10 minutes, plus freezing**

VARIATION
For a melon and almond smoothie, blend 2/3 cup frozen galia melon flesh with 1/2 cup chilled, sweetened almond milk.

AFFORDABILITY 1

Cucumber LASSI Ⓥ

½ cucumber
⅔ cup plain yogurt
½ cup ice cold water
handful of mint
½ teaspoon ground cumin
squeeze of lemon juice

Serves **1**
Prep time **10 minutes**

1 Peel and coarsely chop the cucumber. Put it into a blender or food processor with the yogurt and iced water.

2 Pull the mint leaves off their stems, reserving a few for decoration. Chop the remainder coarsely and put into the blender. Add the cumin and lemon juice and blend briefly until smooth.

3 Pour the smoothie into a glass, decorate with mint leaves, if desired, and serve immediately.

VARIATION
For mango lassi, cut the flesh of 1 ripe mango into cubes and add it to a blender or food processor with ⅔ cup plain yogurt and the same amount of ice cold water, 1 tablespoon rosewater, and ¼ teaspoon ground cardamom. Blend briefly, then serve immediately.

HEALTHY TIP

SMOOTHIE DOES IT If your fruit bowl is looking a little desperate, with a couple of lonely items fast approaching overripeness, wash, peel, dice and slice, and process them up into a liquid vitamin boost. Add a dash of orange juice or other fruit juice if you need to boost the volume.

BERRY, HONEY & YOGURT CUPS Ⓥ

1 Process half of the berries with the orange juice and honey in a blender or food processor until fairly smooth.

2 Transfer to a bowl and stir in the remaining berries.

3 Divide one-third of the berry mixture among 4 glasses or small bowls. Top with half of the yogurt.

4 Layer with half of the remaining berry mixture and top with the remaining yogurt.

5 Top with the remaining berry mixture, then sprinkle with the granola just before serving.

3½ cups frozen mixed berries, defrosted
juice of 1 orange
⅓ cup honey
1⅔ cups vanilla yogurt
⅓ cup granola

Serves **4**
Prep time **10 minutes**

Blueberry, Oat & Honey
CRISP

1. Put the butter in a 1 cup microwave-proof mug and microwave on full power for 30 seconds or until melted.

2. Stir in the oats, sugar, honey, and cinnamon and microwave on full power for 1 minute.

3. Mix well, then stir in the blueberries and microwave on full power for another 1 minute, until the blueberry juices start to run. Serve with Greek yogurt.

1 tablespoon unsalted butter
2/3 cup rolled oats
1 tablespoon packed light brown sugar
2 teaspoons honey
generous pinch of ground cinnamon
1/3 cup blueberries
nonfat Greek yogurt, to serve

Serves **1**
Prep time **2 minutes**
Cooking time **2½ minutes**

AFFORDABILITY
1

APPLE & YOGURT MUESLI   Ⓥ

AFFORDABILITY **2**

1 Put the muesli into a bowl and mix with the grated apple. Pour the apple juice over the cereal, stir well to combine, and let soak for 5-6 minutes.

2 Divide the soaked muesli between 2 serving bowls and spoon the yogurt on top.

3 Sprinkle with the flaxseed, if using, and serve with a drizzle of honey, if desired.

1 cup fruit and nut muesli, preferably without added sugar
1 tart apple, such as Granny Smith, peeled, cored, and coarsely grated
1 cup chilled apple juice
½ cup nonfat Greek yogurt with honey

To serve
flaxseed (optional)
honey (optional)

Serves **2**
Prep time **10 minutes, plus soaking**

HEALTHY TIP

BULK UP BREAKFAST If you eat a hearty meal before heading to college, you probably won't be tempted as much by unhealthy snacks during the morning. Think big: Oatmeal, granola, or muesli with some chopped fruit and plain yogurt should see you through until lunchtime.

MAPLE-GLAZED GRANOLA
WITH FRUIT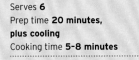

2 tablespoons olive oil
2 tablespoons maple syrup
1/3 cup slivered almonds
1/3 cup pine nuts
3 tablespoons sunflower seeds
1/4 cup rolled oats
1 2/3 cups plain yogurt

Fruit salad
1 ripe mango, peeled, pitted,
   and sliced
2 kiwifruit, peeled and sliced
small bunch of red seedless
   grapes, halved
finely grated zest and juice
   1 lime

Serves **6**
Prep time **20 minutes,**
plus cooling
Cooking time **5-8 minutes**

1 Heat the oil in an ovenproof skillet, then add the maple syrup, nuts, seeds, and oats and toss together.

2 Transfer the pan to a preheated oven, at 350°F, and cook for 5-8 minutes, stirring once and moving the brown edges to the center, until the granola mixture is evenly toasted.

3 Let the mixture cool, then pack it into a storage jar, seal, label, and consume within 10 days.

4 Make the fruit salad. Mix the fruits with the lime zest and juice, spoon the mixture into bowls, and top with spoonfuls of plain yogurt and granola.

MIXED GRAIN PORRIDGE Ⓥ

QUICK AND EASY TO MAKE, THIS BLEND OF QUINOA, BUCKWHEAT, AND MILLET FLAKES PRODUCES A FINISHED PORRIDGE THAT HAS A SLIGHTLY SMOOTHER TEXTURE THAN OATMEAL.

1 Put the grain flakes, milk, and water into a saucepan and bring to a boil, then reduce the heat and cook for 4–5 minutes, stirring, until thickened.

2 Mash 1 of the bananas and slice the other. Stir the mashed banana into the porridge, then spoon into bowls and top with spoonfuls of yogurt, the sliced banana, a drizzle of honey or maple syrup, and a sprinkling of cinnamon. Serve immediately.

NUTRITIONAL TIP
Use unsweetened soy milk instead of dairy milk, if you prefer. If you use soy yogurt instead of Greek yogurt, this dish will be suitable for a dairy-free or vegan diet.

1 cup buckwheat flakes
½ cup quinoa flakes
½ cup millet flakes
2½ cups low-fat milk
1¼ cups water
2 bananas, peeled

To serve
¼ cup nonfat Greek yogurt
honey or maple syrup
sprinkling of ground cinnamon

Serves **4**
Prep time **5 minutes**
Cooking time **4–5 minutes**

PRUNE & BANANA CRUNCH

1   Mix together the banana, prunes, and yogurt in a mixing bowl.

2   Spoon into 2 serving bowls and top with the cornflakes or crunchy cereal flakes. Serve immediately.

1 firm ripe banana, peeled and diced
¾ cup pitted dried prunes
1 cup nonfat Greek yogurt
1½ cups cornflakes or crunchy cereal flakes

Serves **2**
Prep time **5 minutes**

SPICED APPLE
PORRIDGE

1 Put the apple juice and cinnamon into a microwave-proof serving bowl. Sprinkle the millet flakes on top and stir gently.

2 Microwave on full power for 3-4 minutes, stirring frequently, until thick and creamy.

3 Alternatively, put the ingredients into a small saucepan and heat gently for 6-8 minutes, stirring frequently, until thick and creamy. Add a little extra juice if the mixture becomes dry.

4 Serve hot with the yogurt and, if you prefer your porridge sweet, a teaspoon or so of sugar.

VARIATION
For a berry compote, to serve with the granola instead of the fruit salad, put 1 cup each of raspberries, blackberries, and blueberries into a saucepan with the finely grated zest and juice of 1 lemon. Heat gently until the fruit has softened and the blueberries have burst, then sweeten with honey to taste. Serve with the granola and yogurt, as above.

1 cup apple juice
½ teaspoon ground cinnamon
¼ cup millet flakes

To serve
1 tablespoon nonfat Greek yogurt
Demerara sugar (optional)

Serves **1**
Prep time **1 minute**
Cooking time **6-8 minutes**

HEALTHY TIP

DON'T TAKE THE BUS If you live just a few stops from college, there's no excuse for not walking. A brisk walk will get your heart pumping and blood flowing—and reduce the chances that you'll doze off during a lecture.

BANANA & RAISIN PANCAKES

(V)

1 Put the flour, sugar, and baking powder into a mixing bowl. Add the mashed banana with the egg. Gradually whisk in the milk with a fork until the mixture resembles a smooth thick batter. Stir in the raisins.

2 Pour a little oil onto a piece of folded paper towel and use to grease a flat griddle pan or heavy nonstick skillet. Heat the pan, then drop heaping tablespoonfuls of the batter (in batches), well spaced apart, onto the pan. Cook for 2 minutes, until bubbles appear on the top and the undersides are golden. Turn over and cook for another 1-2 minutes, until the second side is done.

3 Serve warm, topped with 1 teaspoon butter, honey, or maple syrup per pancake. These are best eaten on the day they are made.

VARIATION
For summer berry drop pancakes, prepare the recipe as above, but stir in 1 cup mixed fresh blueberries and raspberries instead of the raisins.

1 cup all-purpose flour
2 tablespoons granulated sugar
1½ teaspoons baking powder
1 small ripe banana, peeled and
    coarsely mashed
1 egg, beaten
²/₃ cup milk
¹/₃ cup raisins
vegetable oil, for greasing
butter, honey, or maple syrup,
    to serve

Makes **10**
Prep time **10 minutes**
Cooking time **8 minutes**

CORN & BACON MUFFINS

1 Lightly oil a 12-cup muffin pan.

2 Cut off any rind and excess fat, then finely chop the bacon and dry-fry it in a skillet with the onion over medium heat for 3–4 minutes, until the bacon is turning crisp. Meanwhile, cook the corn in a small saucepan of boiling water for 2 minutes to soften, then drain.

3 Put the cornmeal, flour, and baking powder into a bowl and mix together. Add the corn, bacon, onion, and cheese and stir in.

4 Whisk the milk, eggs, and oil together in a separate bowl, then pour into the flour mixture and stir gently until just combined.

5 Divide the batter among the cups of the prepared muffin pan. Bake in a preheated oven, at 425°F, for 15–20 minutes, until golden and just firm. Loosen the edges of the muffins with a knife and transfer to a wire rack to cool. Serve warm or cold. These are best eaten on the day they are made.

3 tablespoons vegetable oil, plus extra for greasing
6 bacon slices
1 small red onion, finely chopped
1⅓ cups frozen corn kernels
1 cup fine cornmeal
1 cup all-purpose flour
2 teaspoons baking powder
½ cup shredded cheddar cheese
1 cup milk
2 eggs

Makes **12**
Prep time **15 minutes,**
plus cooling
Cooking time **25 minutes**

VARIATION

For spiced corn and scallion muffins, omit the bacon. Prepare the recipe as above, replacing the red onion with 4 scallions, thinly sliced into rounds, and add 1 teaspoon hot paprika and 1 seeded and finely chopped red chile to the mixture before baking.

Very Berry MUFFINS (V)

1. Line a 12-cup muffin pan with nonstick paper liners.

2. Put all the ingredients, except the berries, into a bowl and mix together to make a smooth batter. Fold in the berries.

3. Divide the batter among the paper liners. Bake in a preheated oven, at 350°F, for 25 minutes or until a toothpick comes out clean when inserted. Transfer to a wire rack to cool. Serve warm or cold. These are best eaten on the day they are made.

VARIATION
For banana and pecan muffins, prepare the recipe as above, but use 2 chopped, peeled small bananas instead of the berries (select firm but ripe bananas), adding 1 cup chopped pecans with the bananas. Serve warm, drizzled with maple syrup, if desired.

1 tablespoon baking powder
1 egg, beaten
1 cup milk
¼ cup vegetable oil
1¾ cups coarsely chopped
   mixed fresh berries

Makes **12**
Prep time **15 minutes,**
plus cooling
Cooking time **25 minutes**

AFFORDABILITY 1

TRIPLE CHOCOLATE
PRETZELS Ⓥ

AFFORDABILITY 1

1 Grease 2 large baking sheets.

2 Mix the flour, yeast, sugar, and salt in a mixing bowl. Add the melted butter or oil and gradually mix in the warm water until you have a smooth dough. Knead the dough for 5 minutes on a lightly floured surface until smooth and elastic.

3 Cut the dough into quarters, then cut each quarter into 10 smaller pieces. Shape each piece into a thin rope about 8 inches long. Bend each rope so that it forms a wide arc, then bring one of the ends around in a loop and secure about halfway along the rope. Do the same with the other end, looping it across the first secured end. Repeat with all the pieces of dough.

4 Transfer the pretzels to the prepared baking sheets. Cover loosely with lightly oiled plastic wrap and let rest in a warm place for 30 minutes, until well risen.

5 Make the glaze. Mix the water and salt in a bowl until the salt has dissolved, then brush this over the pretzels. Bake in a preheated oven, at 400°F, for 6-8 minutes, until golden brown. Transfer to a wire rack to cool.

6 Melt the different chocolates in 3 separate heatproof bowls set over saucepans of barely simmering water. Drizzle random lines of semisweet chocolate over the pretzels, using a spoon. Let harden, then repeat with the white and then the milk chocolate. Store in an airtight container for up to 2 days.

VARIATION
For classic pretzels, brush plain pretzels as soon as they come out of the oven with a glaze made by heating 2 teaspoons salt, ½ teaspoon granulated sugar, and 2 tablespoons water in a saucepan until dissolved.

vegetable oil, for greasing
1⅔ cups white bread flour, plus extra for dusting
1 teaspoon active dry yeast
2 teaspoons granulated sugar
large pinch of salt
1 tablespoon butter, melted, or 1 tablespoon sunflower oil
½ cup lukewarm water
3 oz each semisweet, white, and milk chocolate, broken into pieces

Glaze
2 tablespoons water
½ teaspoon salt

Makes **40**
Prep time **30 minutes, plus rising, cooling, and setting**
Cooking time **15 minutes**

Fruited
GRIDDLE CAKES (V)

AFFORDABILITY 2

1 Put the flour and baking powder into a mixing bowl or a food processor. Add the butter and rub in with your fingertips, or process until the mixture resembles fine bread crumbs. Stir in the sugar, dried fruit, spice, and lemon zest. Add the egg, then gradually mix in the milk, if necessary, to make a smooth dough.

2 Knead the dough lightly, then roll out on a lightly floured surface until ¼ inch)thick. Stamp out 2 inch circles, using a fluted round cookie cutter or a glass. Reknead the scraps and continue rolling and stamping out until all the dough has been used.

3 Pour a little oil onto a piece of folded paper towel and use to grease a flat griddle or heavy nonstick skillet. Heat the pan, then add the cakes, in batches, regreasing the griddle or pan as needed, and cook over medium-low heat for about 3 minutes on each side, until golden brown and cooked through.

4 Serve warm, sprinkled with a little extra sugar or spread with butter, if desired. Store in an airtight container for up to 2 days.

VARIATION
For orange and cinnamon griddle cakes, prepare the recipe as above, but use the finely grated zest of ½ orange instead of the lemon, and 1 teaspoon ground cinnamon in place of the allspice.

2 cups all-purpose flour,
  plus extra for dusting
2 teaspoons baking powder
1 stick (4 oz) butter, diced,
  plus extra for spreading
½ cup granulated sugar,
  plus extra for sprinkling
⅓ cup dried currants
⅓ cup golden raisins
1 teaspoon ground allspice
finely grated zest of ½ lemon
1 egg, beaten
1 tablespoon milk, if needed
vegetable oil, for greasing

Serves **30**
Prep time **25 minutes**
Cooking time **18 minutes**

Oatmeal with Prune Compote Ⓥ

1 Put all the compote ingredients into a small saucepan over medium heat. Simmer gently for 10-12 minutes or until softened and slightly sticky. Let cool. (The compote can be prepared in advance and chilled. Remember to remove the cinnamon stick and clove before serving.)

2 Put the milk, water, vanilla extract, cinnamon, and salt into a large saucepan over medium heat and bring slowly to a boil. Stir in the oats, then reduce the heat and simmer gently, stirring occasionally, for 8-10 minutes, until creamy and tender.

3 Spoon the oatmeal into bowls, sprinkle with the almonds, and serve with the prune compote.

VARIATION

For sweet quinoa porridge with banana and dates, put 1½ cups quinoa into a saucepan with the milk, 1 tablespoon agave nectar or honey, and 2-3 cardamom pods, crushed. Simmer gently for 12-15 minutes or until the quinoa is cooked and the desired consistency is reached. Discard the cardamom pods. Serve the porridge in bowls topped with a dollop of plain yogurt, ⅔ cup chopped pitted dates, and sliced banana.

3¾ cups skim or low-fat milk
2 cups water
1 teaspoon vanilla extract
pinch of ground cinnamon
pinch of salt
2¼ cups rolled oats
3 tablespoons slivered almonds, toasted

Compote
1½ cups pitted dried prunes
½ cup apple juice
1 small cinnamon stick
1 whole clove
1 tablespoon honey
1 unpeeled orange quarter

Serves **8**
Prep time **5 minutes**
Cooking time **20-25 minutes**

Whole Wheat
BLUEBERRY PANCAKES
WITH LEMON CURD YOGURT (V)

1 Sift the flours and baking powder into a large bowl, then make a well in the center. Mix together the milk, egg, and honey in a small bowl, then pour into the dry ingredients and whisk until mixed. Stir in 1 cup of the blueberries.

2 Heat the coconut oil in a large skillet, then drop 2 tablespoons of the batter into the pan for each pancake to form 4 and cook for 4-5 minutes, until golden, then turn over and cook for another 2-3 minutes. Remove from the pan and keep warm. Repeat with the remaining batter to make about 12.

3 Mix together the lemon curd and yogurt in a small bowl. Serve the warm pancakes with dollops of the lemon yogurt, sprinkled with the remaining blueberries and drizzled with honey.

1¼ cups whole wheat flour
⅓ cup plus 1 tablespoon
　all-purpose flour
1 teaspoon baking powder
1¼ cups milk
1 egg, beaten
2 tablespoons honey, plus extra
　for drizzling
1¼ cups blueberries
2 tablespoons coconut oil
1 tablespoon lemon curd
½ cup plain yogurt

Serves **4**
Prep time **15 minutes**
Cooking time **25 minutes**

AFFORDABILITY
2

HEALTHY LUNCHES
and snacks

Buying lunches and snacks in the college cafeteria every day can put a serious dent in your finances. Equally, you'll be more tempted to choose unhealthy options when you're in a hurry and need a quick fix for a rumbling stomach. However, if you can get organized and give yourself an extra 5 minutes in the morning, it's easy to throw together a healthy lunch that will keep you going through the afternoon and leave you money to spare at the end of the week.

LOVE YOUR LEFTOVERS

Surely the quickest lunch of all —just make a little extra when you're cooking dinner and put a serving into a container for the next day. This is ideal for pasta, noodles, and rice dishes. Alternatively, if you're cooking pasta for dinner, you could double the amount of pasta; use what you need for your main meal, then let the rest cool down and stir through green or red pesto for lunch the following day.

VEGETABLE PLATTER

Slice up a bundle of vegetable sticks (cucumber, celery, carrot, bell pepper, cauliflower) and cut a pita bread into thin strips. Pack into a plastic container with a mini container of hummus.

GOING GREEN

You can make a salad out of pretty much anything—start with the obvious salad greens, tomato, cucumber, and celery, and liven it up with leftover cooked meat, canned fish, beans, bell peppers, and a simple homemade dressing of olive oil and balsamic vinegar.

WINTER WARMER

A thermos is a good investment for your kitchen. If you make a big batch of soup (see recipes on pages 48–55), you'll have enough lunches for a week. Heat up the amount you need and pour into a flask, then grab a roll or a couple of slices of buttered bread to make a meal of it.

IT'S A WRAP

Wraps are inexpensive, healthy, and versatile. Try these fillings:
- COOKED CHICKEN & PESTO
- CREAM CHEESE, SHREDDED CARROT & LETTUCE
- FALAFEL & HUMMUS
- TUNA, MAYONNAISE & KIDNEY BEANS
- CHICKPEAS (GARBANZO BEANS) WITH DICED RED BELL PEPPER & CUCUMBER

AN EGG-CELLENT IDEA

Tortilla is healthy, filling, and quick to make. Sauté a chopped onion in a medium skillet. Add some chopped, seeded red or yellow bell pepper and zucchini, cooked diced potato, crushed garlic, and chopped tomato. Pour in 4 beaten eggs and cook, stirring. As the eggs start to set, cook for another minute or so, then finish off under a preheated hot broiler for 1–2 minutes. Place a plate over the pan and tip it over so the tortilla lands on the plate. Let cool, then divide into large slices for lunch over the next couple of days or so. See page 72 for an alternative tasty Spinach & Potato Tortilla recipe.

ON-THE-GO
Granola Breakfast Bars

1 Grease a shallow 8 inch square baking pan.

2 Put the butter and honey into a saucepan and bring gently to a boil, stirring continuously, until the mixture bubbles. Add the cinnamon, dried fruit, seeds, and nuts, then stir and heat for 1 minute.

3 Remove from the heat and add the oats. Stir well, then transfer to the prepared pan and press down well. Bake in a preheated oven, at 375°F, for 15 minutes, until the top is just beginning to brown.

4 Let cool in the pan, then cut into 9 squares or bars to serve. Store in an airtight container for up to 2 days.

6 tablespoons butter, plus extra
  for greasing
1/3 cup honey
1/2 teaspoon ground cinnamon
2/3 cup coarsely chopped
  dried apricots
1/3 cup coarsely chopped dried
  papaya or mango
1/3 cup raisins
1/4 cup mixed seeds, such as
  pumpkin, sesame, and sunflower
1/2 cup pecan pieces
12/3 cups rolled oats

Makes **9**
Prep time **15 minutes,
plus cooling**
Cooking time **15 minutes**

FRUITY MANGO OAT BARS (V)

1 Put the sugar, butter, and syrup into a heavy saucepan and heat gently until melted, then stir in the remaining ingredients until combined.

2 Spoon the batter into an 11 x 7 inch nonstick baking pan lined with parchment paper and press down lightly. Bake in a preheated oven, at 300°F, for 30 minutes or until pale golden brown.

3 Mark into 12 pieces, then cool before removing from the pan. Cut or break into pieces to serve. Store in an airtight container for up to 2 days.

VARIATION

For honey and ginger oat bars, put ¼ cup packed light brown sugar into a saucepan with ¼ cup honey and the butter. Omit the light corn syrup. Heat until melted, then add the millet flakes or 2¼ cups rolled oats and the seeds. Instead of the dried mango, stir in 1 ball of preserved ginger, drained and finely chopped. Spoon the batter into the prepared pan and complete the recipe as above.

½ cup packed light brown sugar
1¼ sticks (5 oz) butter
2 tablespoons light corn syrup
2 cups millet flakes
2 tablespoons mixed seeds, such as pumpkin and sunflower
⅔ cup coarsely chopped dried mango

Makes **12**
Prep time **10 minutes,**
plus cooling
Cooking time **30 minutes**

SEEDED SPELT SODA BREAD (V)

1   Grease a loaf pan with a capacity of at least 3 cups. If you don't have a loaf pan, grease a baking sheet.

2   Sift the flours and baking powder into a bowl. Add the grain left in the sifter and stir in the salt and seeds. Add the buttermilk and milk and mix with a blunt knife to form a soft dough.

3   Turn out onto a lightly floured surface and shape into an oblong. Turn into the prepared pan or neaten the shape and place on the baking sheet. Bake in a preheated oven, at 400°F, for 20 minutes.

4   Reduce the oven temperature to 325°F, and bake for another 15 minutes. Turn out of the pan (if using) and return to the oven shelf for another 10 minutes baking. Let cool completely on a wire rack. Serve in slices. This is best eaten on the day it is made.

vegetable oil, for greasing
2¼ cups spelt flour, plus extra for dusting
1 cup rye flour
2 teaspoons baking powder
1 teaspoon salt
¼ cup pumpkin seeds
¼ cup sunflower seeds
1¼ cups buttermilk
½ cup low-fat milk

Makes **1 loaf; serves 8**
Prep time **10 minutes, plus cooling**
Cooking time **45 minutes**

AFFORDABILITY
1

STUDENT TIP

BREAD CRUMBS When you get to the last slices of bread, don't throw them away if they are too dry; process in a blender and keep the bread crumbs in an airtight container in the freezer. They're great for casserole toppings.

FALAFEL PITA POCKETS

1. Put the chickpeas into a bowl, add cold water to cover by a generous 4 inches, and let soak overnight.

2. Drain the chickpeas, transfer to a blender or food processor, and process until coarsely ground. Add the onion, garlic, fresh herbs, ground coriander, and baking powder. Season with salt and black pepper and process until really smooth. Using wet hands, shape the mixture into 16 small patties.

3. Heat the oil in a large skillet over medium-high heat, add the patties, in batches, and cook for 3 minutes on each side or until golden and cooked through. Remove with a slotted spoon and drain on paper towels.

4. Halve the pita breads and fill with the falafel, salad greens, and diced tomatoes. Add a spoonful of the yogurt to each and serve immediately.

VARIATION

For a falafel salad, toss 4 handfuls of mixed salad greens with a little olive oil, lemon juice, and salt and black pepper and arrange on serving plates. Core, seed, and dice 1 red bell pepper and sprinkle it over the salads. Top with the falafel and spoon over a little plain or nonfat Greek yogurt.

1⅓ cups dried chickpeas (garbanzo beans)
1 small onion, finely chopped
2 garlic cloves, crushed
½ bunch of parsley
½ bunch of fresh cilantro
2 teaspoons ground coriander
½ teaspoon baking powder
2 tablespoons vegetable oil
4 whole wheat pita breads
handful of salad greens
2 tomatoes, diced
¼ cup nonfat Greek yogurt
salt and black pepper

Serves **4**
Prep time **15 minutes,
plus overnight soaking**
Cooking time **12 minutes**

FALAFELS WITH BEET SALAD & MINT YOGURT (V)

1 To make the falafels, put the chickpeas, onion, garlic, chile, cumin, coriander, and parsley into a blender or food processor. Season with salt and black pepper, then process to make a coarse paste. Shape the mixture into 8 patties and set aside.

2 To make the salad, put the carrot, beet, and spinach into a bowl. Season with salt and black pepper, add the lemon juice and oil, and stir well.

3 To make the mint yogurt, mix all the ingredients together in a small bowl and season with a little salt.

4 Heat the oil in a skillet, add the falafels, and cook for 4-5 minutes on each side, until golden. Serve with the beet salad and mint yogurt.

Falafels
1 (15 oz) can chickpeas (garbanzo beans), rinsed and drained
½ small red onion, coarsely chopped
1 garlic clove, chopped
½ red chile, seeded
1 teaspoon ground cumin
1 teaspoon ground coriander
handful of flat leaf parsley
2 tablespoons olive oil
salt and black pepper

Beet salad
1 carrot, shredded
1 raw beet, shredded
2 cups baby spinach leaves
1 tablespoon lemon juice
2 tablespoons olive oil

Mint yogurt
⅔ cup nonfat Greek yogurt
1 tablespoon chopped mint leaves
½ garlic clove, crushed

Serves **2**
Prep time **20 minutes**
Cooking time **10 minutes**

Brown Rice Salad
WITH PEANUTS & RAISINS

Vegan

1 Cook the rice in a saucepan of lightly salted boiling water for 15-18 minutes, or according to the package directions, until tender.

2 Meanwhile, put the scallions, raisins, red bell pepper, and peanuts into a large bowl and toss with the soy sauce and oil until well coated.

3 Once the rice is cooked, drain it in a strainer and rinse with cold water until cold. Once cold and drained, add to the other ingredients and toss well to coat and mix.

4 Turn into a serving bowl and serve, or put into a lunch box with slices of cheese or meat to serve alongside, if desired.

1 cup quick-cooking brown rice
bunch of scallions, coarsely chopped
1 cup raisins
1 red bell pepper, cored, seeded, and sliced
½ cup roasted peanuts
2 tablespoons dark soy sauce
1 tablespoon sesame oil
salt

Serves **4**
Prep time **10 minutes**
Cooking time **18 minutes**

AFFORDABILITY
1

HEALTHY TIP

GO NUTS FOR NUTS Although the ultimate healthy snack, nuts can be expensive, so buy a huge package and divide into smaller portions to save money. Go for unsalted/unflavored (natural) nuts and don't forget seeds (such as sunflower, pumpkin, and flaxseed) for a healthy snack that is great for sprinkling.

PORK & APPLE BALLS

1. Put the apple and onion into a bowl with the ground pork and, using a fork, mash all the ingredients together well. Shape into 16 coarse balls. Place the bread crumbs on a plate and roll the balls in the bread crumbs to lightly coat them all over.

2. Heat the oil in a large, heavy skillet and cook the pork balls over medium-high heat for 8-10 minutes, turning frequently, until cooked through. Drain on paper towels.

3. Serve warm with tomato relish and cherry tomatoes, and provide bamboo paddle skewers or forks for dipping the balls in the relish.

1 small crisp, sweet apple, such as McIntosh, cored and grated (with skin on)
1 small onion, grated
8 oz ground pork
1 cup fresh whole wheat bread crumbs
3 tablespoons vegetable oil

To serve
tomato relish
cherry tomatoes

Serves **4**
Prep time **15 minutes**
Cooking time **10 minutes**

Sweet Potato & Bean
ASIAN "BUNS"

Vegan

1. Mix the zucchini with the sugar and 2 teaspoons of the vinegar in a small bowl and let stand while preparing the filling.

2. Thinly slice the sweet potatoes and cook in a saucepan of boiling water for 8–10 minutes, until just tender. Add the beans and cook for another 2 minutes to soften. Drain.

3. Add the hoisin sauce and the remaining vinegar to the saucepan. Add the drained vegetables, scallions, and cilantro and mix well.

4. Wrap the pita breads in plastic wrap and microwave on full power for 1–2 minutes, until soft.

5. Halve the pita breads and fill with the sweet potato mixture. Spoon the zucchini mixture on top, then serve.

1 cup shredded zucchini
1 teaspoon granulated sugar
3 teaspoons rice vinegar
2 sweet potatoes, scrubbed
1 cup trimmed 1 inch green bean
  pieces
¼ cup hoisin sauce
4 scallions, thinly sliced
¼ cup chopped fresh cilantro
2 whole wheat or white
  pita breads

Serves **2**
Prep time **15 minutes**
Cooking time **14 minutes**

TUNA & CORN WRAPS

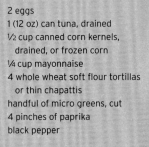

1 Place the eggs in a saucepan of water and bring to a boil. Reduce the heat and simmer for 10 minutes, until hard-boiled. Remove from the pan and plunge into cold water to cool.

2 Meanwhile, put the tuna and corn kernels into a mixing bowl and season with black pepper. Add the mayonnaise and mix together.

3 Lay the tortillas or chapattis on a cutting board and divide the tuna mixture between them, piling it across the middle of each. Shell the eggs and coarsely chop, then sprinkle them over the tuna mixture. Sprinkle with the greens. Sprinkle each with a pinch of paprika, then roll up tightly and cut in half to serve. Wrap in wax paper to travel, if desired.

2 eggs
1 (12 oz) can tuna, drained
½ cup canned corn kernels, drained, or frozen corn
¼ cup mayonnaise
4 whole wheat soft flour tortillas or thin chapattis
handful of micro greens, cut
4 pinches of paprika
black pepper

Serves **4**
Prep time **15 minutes**
Cooking time **15 minutes**

Mushroom & Arugula
SEEDED WRAP
WITH FETA & GARLIC DRESSING (V)

1   Add the crumbled feta cheese to a small bowl and stir in
    the yogurt. Season with plenty of black pepper and beat
    well with a fork.

2   Heat the oil in a small skillet and sauté the mushrooms for
    about 5 minutes, until beginning to brown and the juices
    have evaporated. Stir in the garam masala and a pinch of
    salt and cook for another 2 minutes.

3   Lightly broil the wrap under a preheated hot broiler until
    warmed through. Spread with the feta mixture and sprinkle
    the mushrooms on top. Sprinkle with the bean sprouts and
    arugula and drizzle with the honey. Roll up loosely to serve.

⅓ cup crumbled feta cheese
¼ cup nonfat Greek yogurt
1 tablespoon vegetable oil
3 cups trimmed and thinly sliced
  button mushrooms
½ teaspoon garam masala
1 seeded wrap
¼ cup bean sprouts
small handful of arugula
1 teaspoon honey
salt and black pepper

Serves **1**
Prep time **5 minutes**
Cooking time **8 minutes**

BLACKENED TOFU WRAPS Ⓥ

AFFORDABILITY 1

7 oz tofu
1 tablespoon packed
   dark brown sugar
1 teaspoon black pepper
1 teaspoon five-spice powder
½ teaspoon ground ginger
1 garlic clove, crushed
2 seeded wraps
2 tablespoons sesame oil
2 cups mixed salad greens
1 carrot, grated
½ bunch of scallions, thinly sliced
1 tablespoon honey
squeeze of lime or lemon juice
salt

Serves **2**
Prep time **10 minutes**
Cooking time **5 minutes**

1 Thoroughly drain the tofu between several sheets of paper towels. Cut into thin slices. Mix together the sugar, black pepper, five-spice powder, ginger, and a little salt. Spread the garlic over the tofu, then dust on both sides with the spice mixture.

2 Warm the wraps in a skillet or under a preheated hot broiler.

3 Heat 1 tablespoon of the oil in a skillet and sauté the tofu slices for 1-2 minutes on each side, until deep golden.

4 Sprinkle the salad greens, carrot, and scallions over the warm wraps, then place the tofu slices on top, positioning them over the length of the wraps.

5 Add the remaining oil, the honey, and lime or lemon juice to the pan and stir to mix. Drizzle the dressing over the wraps, roll, and then serve warm or cold.

Healthy & Hearty

TAGLIATELLE WITH PUMPKIN & SAGE

HEARTY
MINESTRONE (V)

1 Process the carrots, onion, and celery in a blender or food processor until finely chopped.

2 Heat the oil in a large saucepan, then add the chopped vegetables, garlic, potatoes, tomato paste, broth, tomatoes, and pasta. Bring to a boil, then reduce the heat and simmer, covered, for 12-15 minutes, stirring occasionally.

3 Add in the white kidney beans and spinach for the final 2 minutes of the cooking time.

4 Season to taste with salt and black pepper and serve with crusty bread.

3 carrots, coarsely chopped
1 red onion, coarsely chopped
6 celery sticks, coarsely chopped
2 tablespoons olive oil
2 garlic cloves, crushed
2 potatoes, such as Yukon gold or white rounds, peeled and cut into ½ inch dice
¼ cup tomato paste
6½ cups Vegetable Broth (see page 244)
1 (14½ oz) can diced tomatoes
5 oz short soup pasta shapes
1 (15 oz) can white kidney (cannellini) beans, rinsed and drained
3½ cups baby spinach
salt and black pepper
crusty bread, to serve

Serves **4**
Prep time **10 minutes**
Cooking time **20 minutes**

HEALTHY TIP

WISE UP TO WATER It really is the elixir of life, so try to make sure you drink more aqua than sugary drinks. Keep a bottle in your bag and drink regularly throughout the day to keep your brain alert and lethargy at bay.

Summer
VEGETABLE SOUP

1 Heat the oil in a medium saucepan and sauté the leek for 3-4 minutes, until softened. Add the potato and broth to the pan and cook for 10 minutes. Add the mixed summer vegetables and the mint, then bring to a boil. Reduce the heat and simmer, stirring occasionally, for 10 minutes.

2 Cool slightly, then transfer the soup to a blender or food processor and puree until smooth. Return the soup to the pan, add the sour cream, and season to taste with salt and black pepper. Heat through gently and serve.

VARIATION
For chunky summer vegetable soup with mixed herb gremolata, make up the soup as above but do not puree. Ladle the soup into bowls and serve topped with 2 tablespoons of sour cream and gremolata, made by mixing together 2 tablespoons chopped basil, 2 tablespoons chopped parsley, the finely grated zest of 1 lemon, and 1 finely chopped small garlic clove.

1 teaspoon olive oil
1 leek, trimmed, cleaned and thinly sliced
1 large potato, such as Yukon gold or white rounds, peeled and chopped
4 cups Vegetable Broth (see page 244)
4 cups prepared mixed summer vegetables, such as peas, asparagus, fava beans, and zucchini
2 tablespoons chopped mint
2 tablespoons reduced-fat sour cream
salt and black pepper

Serves **4**
Prep time **15 minutes**
Cooking time **30 minutes**

RED PEPPER & ZUCCHINI
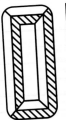

SOUP (V)

AFFORDABILITY 3

1 Heat the oil in a large saucepan and gently sauté the onions for 5 minutes or until softened and golden brown. Add the garlic and cook gently for 1 minute. Add the red bell peppers and half of the zucchini to the pan. Sauté for 5-8 minutes or until softened and brown.

2 Add the broth to the pan, season to taste with salt and black pepper, and bring to a boil. Reduce the heat, cover the pan, and simmer gently, stirring occasionally, for 20 minutes.

3 Let the soup cool slightly once the vegetables are tender, then puree, in batches, in a blender or food processor. Gently sauté the remaining chopped zucchini for 5 minutes (you may need to add a little more oil to the pan).

4 Meanwhile, return the soup to the pan, reheat gently, then taste and adjust the seasoning, if needed. Serve topped with the fried zucchini, yogurt or sour cream, and chives.

VARIATION
For red pepper and carrot soup, make up the soup as above, adding 2 diced carrots instead of the zucchini, plus the red bell peppers, to the sautéed onion and garlic. Continue as above. Puree, reheat, and serve topped with teaspoonfuls of garlic and herb cream cheese and some snipped chives.

2 tablespoons olive oil
2 onions, finely chopped
1 garlic clove, crushed
3 red bell peppers, cored, seeded, and coarsely chopped
2 zucchini, coarsely chopped
4 cups Vegetable Broth (see page 244)
salt and black pepper

To serve
low-fat plain yogurt or reduced-fat sour cream
whole chives

Serves **4**
Prep time **15 minutes**
Cooking time **40 minutes**

BEEF

& BARLEY BRÖ

AFFORDABILITY **2**

1 Melt the butter in a large saucepan, then add the beef and onion and sauté for 5 minutes, stirring, until the beef is browned and the onion is just beginning to brown.

2 Stir in the diced vegetables, pearl barley, broth, and mustard, if using. Season with salt and black pepper and bring to a boil. Cover and simmer for 1¾ hours, stirring occasionally, until the meat and vegetables are tender. Taste and adjust the seasoning, if needed.

3 Ladle the soup into bowls and sprinkle with a little chopped parsley just before serving.

VARIATION
For a lamb and barley stew, substitute the beef for 8 oz diced lamb and sauté with the onion as above. Add the sliced white part of 1 trimmed and cleaned leek, 1½ cups diced rutabaga or sweet potato, 2 diced large carrots, and 2 diced Yukon gold or white round potatoes, then mix in ¼ cup pearl barley, 8½ cups lamb broth, 2-3 sprigs of rosemary, and salt and black pepper. Bring to a boil, then cover and simmer for 1¾ hours. Discard the rosemary, add the remaining thinly sliced green leek, and cook for another 10 minutes. Ladle into bowls and sprinkle with a little extra chopped rosemary to serve.

2 tablespoons butter
8 oz chuck shoulder beef, fat trimmed away and meat cut into small cubes
1 large onion, finely chopped
1½ cups diced rutabaga, turnip, or sweet potato
2 large carrots, diced
½ cup pearl barley
8½ cups beef broth
2 teaspoons dry English mustard (optional)
salt and black pepper
chopped parsley, to garnish

Serves **6**
Prep time **20 minutes**
Cooking time **1¾ hours**

BUTTERNUT & ROSEMARY SOUP

Vegan

1   Place the squash pieces in a nonstick roasting pan. Sprinkle the rosemary sprigs over the top and season with salt and black pepper. Roast in a preheated oven, at 400°F, for 45 minutes.

2   Meanwhile, put the lentils into a saucepan and cover with water, then bring to a boil and boil rapidly for 10 minutes. Drain, then return to a clean saucepan with the onion and broth and simmer for 5 minutes. Season with salt and black pepper.

3   Remove the squash from the oven and scoop the flesh from the skin. Mash the flesh with a fork and add it to the soup, then simmer for 25 minutes, stirring occasionally, until the lentils are tender. Serve the soup sprinkled with extra rosemary.

1 butternut squash, halved, seeded, and cut into small chunks
few rosemary sprigs, plus extra leaves to garnish
¾ cup red lentils, rinsed and drained
1 onion, finely chopped
4 cups Vegetable Broth (see page 244)
salt and black pepper

Serves **4**
Prep time **15 minutes**
Cooking time **1 hour 10 minutes**

AFFORDABILITY 1

SQUASH, KALE & MIXED BEAN SOUP ⓥ

1 Heat the oil in a saucepan over medium-low heat, add the onion, and sauté gently for 5 minutes. Stir in the garlic and smoked paprika and cook briefly, then add the squash, carrots, tomatoes, and mixed beans. Pour in the broth, season with salt and black pepper, and bring to a boil, stirring frequently. Reduce the heat, cover, and simmer for 25 minutes, stirring occasionally, until the vegetables are cooked and tender.

2 Stir in the sour cream, then add the kale, pressing it just beneath the surface of the broth. Cover and cook for 5 minutes or until the kale has just wilted. Ladle into bowls and serve with warm garlic bread, if desired.

VARIATION
For cheesy squash, red pepper, and mixed bean soup, make as above, replacing the carrots with 1 cored, seeded, and diced red bell pepper. Pour in the broth, then add ¾ cup Parmesan-style cheese rinds and season. Cover and simmer for 25 minutes. Stir in the sour cream but omit the kale. Discard the cheese rinds, ladle the soup into bowls, and top with grated Parmesan-style cheese.

1 tablespoon olive oil
1 onion, finely chopped
2 garlic cloves, finely chopped
1 teaspoon smoked paprika
½ butternut squash, halved, seeded, peeled, and diced
2 small carrots, peeled and diced
4 tomatoes, skinned (optional) and coarsely chopped
2 cups rinsed and drained mixed canned beans, such as kidney beans, pinto beans, and chickpeas (garbanzo beans)
4 cups Vegetable Broth (see page 244)
⅔ cup reduced-fat sour cream
1½ cups bite-size torn kale pieces
salt and black pepper
crusty bread or warm garlic bread, to serve (optional)

Serves **6**
Prep time **15 minutes**
Cooking time **45 minutes**

AFFORDABILITY 1

Sweet Potato & CABBAGE SOUP

1 Put the onions, garlic, and bacon into a large saucepan and sauté for 2-3 minutes. Add the sweet potatoes, parsnips, thyme, and broth, then bring to a boil and simmer for 15 minutes, stirring occasionally.

2 Cool slightly, then transfer two-thirds of the soup to a blender or food processor and blend until smooth. Return to the pan, add the cabbage, and simmer for 5-7 minutes, until the cabbage is just cooked. Serve with Irish soda bread or whole-grain bread.

VARIATION
For squash and broccoli soup, follow the recipe above, replacing the sweet potatoes with ½ seeded, peeled, and chopped butternut squash. After returning the blended soup to the pan, add 1½ cups small broccoli florets. Cook as above, omitting the cabbage.

2 onions, chopped
2 garlic cloves, sliced
4 slices lean bacon, chopped
3 sweet potatoes, scrubbed or peeled and chopped
2 parsnips, chopped
1 teaspoon chopped thyme
4 cups Vegetable Broth (see page 244)
1 baby savoy cabbage, shredded
Irish soda bread or whole-grain bread, to serve

Serves **4**
Prep time **15 minutes**
Cooking time **25 minutes**

TAGLIATELLE
WITH SQUASH & SAGE (V)

1 Place the squash into a small roasting pan, add 2 tablespoons of the oil, season with salt and black pepper, and toss to mix well. Roast in a preheated oven, at 425°F, for 15-20 minutes or until just tender.

2 Meanwhile, bring a large saucepan of lightly salted water to a boil. Cook the pasta according to the package directions.

3 Drain the pasta, return to the pan, then add the arugula, sage, and roasted squash. Mix together over gentle heat with the remaining oil until the arugula has wilted, then serve with a good grating of cheese, if desired.

1 butternut or other winter squash, peeled, seeded and cut into ¾ inch cubes (3 cups prepared)
¼ cup olive oil
1 lb fresh tagliatelle
2 cups arugula
8 sage leaves, chopped
salt and black pepper
grated Parmesan-style cheese, to serve (optional)

Makes **4**
Prep time **15 minutes**
Cooking time **15-20 minutes**

AFFORDABILITY 1

STUDENT TIP

COMPARE PRICES Every penny counts when you're shopping on a budget, so try out a price comparison site to make sure you're getting the best supermarket deals in your basket.

Eggplant CANNELLONI ⓥ

AFFORDABILITY
3

ALTHOUGH A LITTLE EFFORT IS NECESSARY TO PREPARE, THIS DISH IS WELL WORTH THE TIME, MAKING A DELICIOUS COMBINATION OF CREAMY RICOTTA FILLING AND SWEET, BROILED EGGPLANTS.

1 Bring a large saucepan of lightly salted water to a boil. Add the lasagna noodles, return to a boil, and cook for 2 minutes if fresh or 8–10 minutes if dried. Drain the noodles and immerse in cold water.

2 Place the eggplant slices in a single layer on an aluminum foil-lined broiler rack. (You may need to do this in 2 batches.) Mix together the oil, thyme, and some salt and black pepper and brush the seasoning over the eggplants. Broil under a preheated medium-hot broiler until lightly browned all over, turning once.

3 Beat the ricotta in a bowl with the basil, garlic, and a little salt and black pepper. Thoroughly drain the pasta noodles and lay them on the work surface. Cut each one in half. Spread the ricotta mixture over the noodles, right to the edges. Arrange the eggplant slices on top. Roll up each pasta noodle to enclose the filling inside.

4 Spread two-thirds of the tomato sauce in a shallow ovenproof dish and arrange the cannelloni on top. Spoon the remaining tomato sauce on top and then sprinkle with the cheese. Bake in a preheated oven, at 375°F, for 20 minutes or until the cheese is golden.

4 fresh or dried lasagna noodles, each about 7 x 6 inches
2 medium eggplants, thinly sliced
¼ cup olive oil
1 teaspoon finely chopped thyme
1 cup ricotta cheese
1 cup basil leaves, torn into pieces
2 garlic cloves, crushed
1 quantity Fresh Tomato Sauce (see page 249)
1 cup shredded fontina or Gruyère cheese
salt and black pepper

Serves **4**
Prep time **30 minutes**
Cooking time **50 minutes**

SPAGHETTI CARBONARA

IT'S THE HEAT FROM THE STEAMING HOT SPAGHETTI THAT LIGHTLY COOKS THE CREAMY EGG SAUCE IN THIS RECIPE. THIS IS A QUICKLY ASSEMBLED DISH (MAKE SURE YOU HAVE EVERYTHING READY BEFORE YOU BEGIN).

1 Beat together the egg yolks, whole eggs, cream, Parmesan, and plenty of black pepper.

2 Heat the oil in a large skillet and cook the pancetta or bacon for 3-4 minutes or until golden and turning crisp. Add the garlic and cook for another 1 minute.

3 Meanwhile, bring a large saucepan of lightly salted water to a boil, add the spaghetti, and cook for 2 minutes, or according to the package directions, until tender.

4 Drain the spaghetti and immediately add to the skillet. Turn off the heat and stir in the egg mixture until the eggs are lightly cooked. Serve immediately. (If the heat of the pasta doesn't quite cook the egg sauce, turn on the heat and cook gently and briefly, stirring.)

4 egg yolks
2 eggs
²/₃ cup light cream
²/₃ cup grated Parmesan cheese
2 tablespoons olive oil
3¹/₂ oz pancetta or streaky bacon, thinly sliced
2 garlic cloves, crushed
1 lb fresh spaghetti
salt and black pepper

Serves **4**
Prep time **10 minutes**
Cooking time **5 minutes**

LINGUINE
WITH SHREDDED HAM & EGGS

1 Bring a large saucepan of lightly salted water to a boil to cook the pasta. Meanwhile, mix together the parsley, mustard, lemon juice, sugar, oil, and a little salt and black pepper. Roll up the ham and slice it as thinly as possible. Trim the scallions, cut them lengthwise into thin shreds, then cut into 2 inch lengths.

2 Put the eggs into a small saucepan and just cover with cold water. Bring to a boil and cook for 4 minutes.

3 Add the pasta to the large saucepan of boiling water, return to a boil, and cook for 6-8 minutes, or according to package directions, until just tender. Add the scallions and cook for another 30 seconds.

4 Drain the pasta and return to the pan. Stir in the ham and the mustard dressing and then pile onto serving plates. Shell and halve the eggs and serve on top.

VARIATION
This recipe is conveniently adaptable. You can use other shredded, cooked meats instead of the ham, such as chicken, turkey, or pork, if you prefer.

4 oz dried linguine
3 tablespoons chopped
 flat leaf parsley
1 tablespoon whole-grain mustard
2 teaspoons lemon juice
good pinch of granulated sugar
3 tablespoons olive oil
4 oz thinly sliced ham
2 scallions
2 eggs
salt and black pepper

Serves **2**
Prep time **5 minutes**
Cooking time **10 minutes**

RAGU SAUCE

RAGU, OR BOLOGNESE, IS USUALLY SERVED WITH TAGLIATELLE. IT SHOULD BE THICK AND PULPY SO IT CLINGS TO THE PASTA IT'S SERVED WITH. IN ITALY, A RAGU SAUCE IS TOSSED WITH THE PASTA INSTEAD OF SPOONED ON TOP.

1 Melt the butter with the oil in a large, heavy saucepan and gently sauté the onion for 5 minutes. Add the celery and carrot and sauté gently for another 2 minutes.

2 Stir in the garlic, then add the ground beef. Cook gently, breaking up the meat, until lightly browned.

3 Add the wine and let the mixture simmer until the wine reduces slightly. Stir in the diced tomatoes, tomato paste, oregano, and bay leaves and bring to a boil.

4 Reduce the heat and cook gently, uncovered, for about 45 minutes, stirring occasionally, until the sauce is thick and pulpy. Remove the bay leaves. Check and adjust the seasoning, then serve with grated Parmesan, if desired.

1 tablespoon butter
3 tablespoons olive oil
1 large onion, finely chopped
1 celery stick, finely chopped
1 carrot, finely chopped
3 garlic cloves, crushed
1 lb ground round beef
2/3 cup red wine
2 (14½ oz) cans diced tomatoes
2 tablespoons tomato paste
3 tablespoons chopped oregano
3 bay leaves
salt and black pepper
grated Parmesan cheese, to serve
  (optional)

Serves **4**
Prep time **15 minutes**
Cooking time **1 hour**

AFFORDABILITY

HEALTHY TIP

GET SAUCY Store-bought sauces can be expensive and many contain more sugar per portion than a worker's first cup of joe of the day. For the cost of a few cans of diced tomatoes and some garlic and herbs, you can cook up a batch of sauce that's healthier and a whole lot cheaper.

TUNA LAYERED LASAGNE

1. Cook the pasta noodles, in batches, in a large saucepan of lightly salted boiling water according to the package directions until al dente. Drain and return to the pan to keep warm.

2. Meanwhile, heat the oil in a skillet over medium heat, add the scallions and zucchini, and cook, stirring, for 3 minutes. Remove the pan from the heat, add the tomatoes, tuna, and arugula, and gently toss everything together.

3. Place a little of the tuna mixture on 4 serving plates and top each portion with a pasta noodle. Spoon the remaining tuna mixture over the pasta, then top with the remaining noodles. Season with black pepper and top each with a spoonful of pesto and some basil leaves before serving.

VARIATION

For salmon lasagne, use 14 oz fresh salmon fillets. Pan-fry the fish for 2-3 minutes on each side or until they are cooked through. Remove the bones and skin, then flake the fish and use in place of the tuna.

8 dried lasagna noodles
1 tablespoon olive oil
bunch of scallions, sliced
2 zucchini, diced
3½ cups quartered cherry tomatoes (about 1 lb)
2 (5 oz) cans tuna in water, drained
2½ cups arugula
4 teaspoons Pesto (see page 248)
salt and black pepper
basil leaves, to garnish

Serves **4**
Prep time **10 minutes**
Cooking time **10 minutes**

TUNA & OLIVE PASTA

1   Heat the oil in a large skillet or saucepan and cook the onion over medium heat for 6-7 minutes, until it begins to soften. Add the garlic and cook for another 1 minute. Pour the diced tomatoes into the pan with the dried red pepper flakes, if using. Simmer gently for 8-10 minutes, stirring occasionally, until thickened slightly.

2   Meanwhile, bring a large saucepan of lightly salted water to a boil and cook the pasta for 10-12 minutes, or according to the package directions, until just tender. Drain and return to the pan. Stir the tomato sauce into the pasta with the tuna and olives and then pile into 4 dishes to serve.

3 tablespoons olive oil or vegetable oil
1 red onion, sliced
2 garlic cloves, chopped
2 (14½ oz) cans diced tomatoes
½ teaspoon dried red pepper flakes (optional)
1 lb pasta shapes, such as penne
1 (5 oz) can tuna in water or oil, drained and flaked
¾ cup pitted black ripe or green olives, drained and coarsely chopped
salt

Serves **4**
Prep time **10 minutes**
Cooking time **20 minutes**

AFFORDABILITY
1

Salmon
WITH GREEN VEGETABLES

1 Heat the oil in a large, heavy skillet and cook the leek over medium heat, stirring frequently, for 3 minutes, until softened. Add the broth, then bring to a boil and continue boiling for 2 minutes, until reduced a little. Add the sour cream and stir well to mix. Add the peas, edamame or fava beans, and salmon and return to a boil.

2 Reduce the heat, cover, and simmer for 10 minutes, until the fish is opaque and cooked through and the peas and beans are piping hot.

3 Sprinkle with the chives and serve spooned over creamy mashed potatoes with a good grinding of black pepper.

1 tablespoon olive oil
1 leek, trimmed, cleaned, and thinly sliced
1 cup fish broth
1 cup reduced-fat sour cream
1 cup frozen peas
1 cup frozen edamame (soybeans) or fava beans
4 chunky skinless salmon fillets, about 5 oz each
2 tablespoons snipped chives

To serve
mashed potatoes
black pepper

Serves **4**
Prep time **10 minutes**
Cooking time **15 minutes**

TUNA & JALAPEÑO BAKED POTATOES

1 Prick the potatoes all over with the tip of a sharp knife and place directly in a preheated oven, at 350°F, for 1 hour or until crisp on the outside and tender inside. Let stand until cool enough to handle.

2 Cut the potatoes in half and scoop the cooked flesh into a bowl. Place the empty potato skins, cut side up, on a baking sheet. Mix the tuna, jalapeño peppers, scallions, tomatoes, and chives into the potato flesh in the bowl. Gently fold in the sour cream, then season to taste with salt and black pepper.

3 Spoon the filling into the potato skins, sprinkle with the cheese, and cook under a preheated medium-hot broiler for 4-5 minutes or until hot and the cheese has melted. Serve immediately with a green salad.

VARIATION

For spicy tuna wraps, spoon ¼ cup chunky spicy tomato salsa onto 4 large, whole wheat soft flour tortillas. Sprinkle with the tuna, jalapeño peppers, and scallions. Omit the tomatoes, chives, and cheese and top with ½ shredded iceberg lettuce. Roll up the wraps tightly and cut in half diagonally. Serve with a little sour cream, if desired.

4 large baking potatoes
2 (5 oz) cans tuna in spring water, drained
2 tablespoons drained and chopped green jalapeño peppers in liquid
2 scallions, finely chopped
4 firm ripe tomatoes, seeded and chopped
2 tablespoons snipped chives
3 tablespoons reduced-fat sour cream
1 cup shredded reduced-fat sharp cheddar-style cheese
salt and black pepper
green salad, to serve

Serves **4**
Prep time **10 minutes, plus cooling**
Cooking time **1 hour 5 minutes**

AFFORDABILITY 1

MACARONI & CHEESE
SURPRISE

1. Cook the macaroni in a large saucepan of lightly salted boiling water according to the package directions until just tender, then drain.

2. Meanwhile, lightly steam all the vegetables in a steamer or colander over a separate saucepan of boiling water for a few minutes so that they remain crunchy. Drain well.

3. Mix the cornstarch and a little of the milk together in a saucepan. Blend to a smooth paste. Add the rest of the milk, then heat gently, whisking continuously until the sauce boils and thickens. Add three-quarters of the cheese, the mustard, and cayenne pepper to taste.

4. Mix together the pasta, vegetables, and sauce and spoon into an ovenproof dish. Sprinkle with the remaining cheese and sprinkle with a little cayenne pepper to garnish. Bake in a preheated oven, at 400°F, for about 25 minutes, until golden brown.

VARIATION
Try adding any vegetables, lightly cooked, to the cheesy mixture, such as peas, corn, mixed bell peppers, carrots, mushrooms, and mixed vegetables.

6 oz whole wheat macaroni
2 carrots, cut into small, chunky sticks
3½ cups broccoli florets
1 large leek, trimmed, cleaned, and thickly sliced
⅓ cup cornstarch
2½ cups skim milk
1 cups shredded reduced-fat sharp cheddar-style cheese
1 teaspoon mustard
pinch of cayenne pepper, plus extra to garnish
salt

Serves **4**
Prep time **15 minutes**
Cooking time **40 minutes**

HEALTHY TIP

All pasta is naturally healthy—rich in carbohydrates and low in fat. Whole wheat pasta is made from the whole grain and contains more insoluble fiber than the white variety. This type of fiber helps to prevent constipation and other bowel problems.

AFFORDABILITY
1

White Bean Gnocchi
WITH SPINACH & PINE NUTS

1 Put the drained beans into a bowl, then mash with a potato masher or a fork. Beat in the garlic, flour, rosemary, and a little salt and black pepper. Mix to a thick paste and then turn out onto the work surface. Divide the mixture in half and roll out each piece into a 14 inch rope shape. Cut across into ¾ inch pieces.

2 Bring a large saucepan of lightly salted water to a boil. Add the bean gnocchi and cook for 2-3 minutes, until the pieces rise to the surface. Remove with a slotted spoon and drain.

3 Heat the oil in a skillet and cook the pine nuts, stirring until lightly browned. Stir in the water and then add the spinach. Heat gently, turning the spinach in the juices until just beginning to wilt.

4 Dot the cheese into the pan and add the gnocchi. Heat through gently, stirring until the cheese has started to melt. Serve immediately.

1 (15 oz) can white kidney (cannellini) beans, rinsed and thoroughly drained
1 garlic clove, crushed
⅓ cup all-purpose flour
1 teaspoon finely chopped rosemary
1 tablespoon olive oil
3 tablespoons pine nuts
3 tablespoons water
1 (10 oz) package spinach, thawed if frozen
⅓ cup crumbled Gorgonzola or other blue cheese
salt and black pepper

Serves **2**
Prep time **20 minutes**
Cooking time **8 minutes**

GNOCCHI VERDE (V)

AFFORDABILITY
2

THIS TYPE OF GNOCCHI, SOMETIMES KNOWN AS ROMAN GNOCCHI, USES A SEMOLINA BASE INSTEAD OF THE MORE FAMILIAR POTATO. IT'S SOFT AND CREAMY COMFORT FOOD.

1 Grease a 12 x 9 inch or similar-size baking dish with butter and line with nonstick parchment paper.

2 Put the milk into a large saucepan and bring to a boil. When the milk starts to boil, lower the heat and sprinkle in the semolina flour, in a steady stream, whisking well until the mixture is thick. Continue beating until the mixture is almost too thick to beat and starts to come away from the sides of the pan.

3 Remove the pan from the heat. Dot with 2 tablespoons of the butter, then add half of the cheese followed by the egg yolks. Season with salt and black pepper and beat until combined. Turn the dough into the prepared pan and spread in an even layer with the back of a spoon or spatula. Let stand for at least 30 minutes, until cool and set.

4 Put the spinach into the cleaned pan with the water and a generous sprinkling of nutmeg. Cover and cook briefly until the spinach has wilted. Drain well, squeezing out any excess water.

5 Use a 2 inch round cutter to cut the semolina dough into circles. Chop the scraps and sprinkle them into a shallow 3½ quart ovenproof dish. Spoon the wilted spinach on top. Arrange the gnocchi circles, slightly overlapping, on top.

6 Melt the remaining butter in a skillet and sauté the shallots until softened. Stir in the cream and spoon the sauce over the gnocchi. Sprinkle with the remaining cheese and bake in a preheated oven, at 400°F, for 20 minutes, until pale golden.

6 tablespoons butter, plus extra for greasing
4 cups milk
1¼ cups semolina flour
1¼ cups grated Parmesan-style cheese
3 egg yolks
1 (12 oz) package baby spinach
1 tablespoon water
plenty of freshly grated nutmeg
2 shallots, finely chopped
⅔ cup light cream
salt and black pepper

Serves **4**
Prep time **50 minutes, plus cooling**
Cooking time **30 minutes**

RANCH-STYLE EGGS

1 Heat the oil in a large skillet and add the onion, chile, garlic, cumin, and oregano. Sauté gently for about 5 minutes or until soft, then add the tomatoes and bell peppers and cook for another 5 minutes. If the sauce looks dry, add a splash of water.

2 Season well with salt and black pepper, then make 4 hollows in the mixture, break an egg into each, and cover the pan. Cook for 5 minutes or until the eggs are just set.

3 Serve immediately, garnished with chopped cilantro.

2 tablespoons olive oil
1 onion, thinly sliced
1 red chile, seeded and
  finely chopped
1 garlic clove, crushed
1 teaspoon ground cumin
1 teaspoon dried oregano
1 (15 oz) can cherry tomatoes
1 cup coarsely chopped, drained
  roasted red and yellow peppers
  in oil (from a jar)
4 eggs
salt and black pepper
¼ cup finely chopped fresh
  cilantro, to garnish

Serves **4**
Prep time **10 minutes**
Cooking time **15 minutes**

AFFORDABILITY
1

SPINACH & BUTTERNUT LASAGNE

V

AFFORDABILITY 2

2 tablespoons olive oil
1 small butternut squash, halved, seeded, peeled, and cut into small dice
1 teaspoon ground cumin
1/4 teaspoon dried red pepper flakes
1 (14 1/2 oz) can diced tomatoes
1 teaspoon granulated sugar
7 cups spinach
1 1/2 tablespoons butter
2 tablespoons all-purpose flour
1 1/4 cups low-fat milk
1 cup shredded sharp cheddar-style cheese
4 oz dried lasagna noodles
salt and black pepper
green salad, to serve

Serves **4**
Prep time **25 minutes**
Cooking time **40 minutes**

1 Heat the oil in a saucepan and gently sauté the squash for 5 minutes, stirring. Add the cumin, dried red pepper flakes, tomatoes, and sugar and simmer gently, uncovered, for 20 minutes, stirring occasionally until the squash is tender. Stir in the spinach until wilted and season to taste with salt and black pepper. Remove from the heat.

2 Melt the butter in a separate saucepan and stir in the flour, beating with a wooden spoon for 1 minute. Gradually stir in the milk and cook over gentle heat, stirring continuously, until thickened and smooth. Beat in half of the cheese and season to taste with salt and black pepper. Remove from the heat.

3 Spread one-quarter of the squash mixture into a shallow, ovenproof dish and cover with a layer of the lasagna noodles, breaking them to fit, if needed. Add another quarter of the squash mixture, spoon over about one-third of the cheese sauce, and cover with another layer of the noodles. Continue layering the ingredients in the same way, finishing with a layer of squash mixture topped with cheese sauce. Sprinkle with the remaining grated cheese.

4 Bake in a preheated oven, at 375°F, for 40 minutes, until golden and bubbling. Serve with a green salad.

SPINACH & POTATO
TORTILLA

1 Heat the oil in a nonstick, ovenproof skillet and add the onions and potatoes. Cook over medium heat for 3-4 minutes or until the vegetables have softened but not browned, turning and stirring often. Add the garlic, spinach, and roasted peppers and stir to mix well.

2 Beat the eggs lightly in a small bowl and season well with salt and black pepper. Pour the eggs into the skillet, shaking the pan so that the egg mixture is evenly spread. Cook gently for 8-10 minutes or until the tortilla is set on the bottom.

3 Sprinkle with the grated cheese. Place the skillet under a preheated medium-hot broiler and cook for 3-4 minutes or until the top is set and golden.

4 Remove from the heat, cut into 4 wedges, and serve warm or at room temperature.

3 tablespoons olive oil
2 onions, finely chopped
1¼ cups cooked peeled potatoes (½ inch cubes)
2 garlic cloves, finely chopped
1 cup coarsely chopped, thoroughly drained cooked spinach
¼ cup finely chopped, drained roasted red peppers in oil (from a jar)
5 eggs
3-4 tablespoons grated Manchego-style cheese
salt and black pepper

Serves **4**
Prep time **10 minutes**
Cooking time **20 minutes**

BUTTERNUT SQUASH & RICOTTA
FRITTATA

1 Heat the oil in a large, deep, ovenproof skillet over medium-low heat, add the onion and butternut squash, then cover loosely and cook gently, stirring frequently, for 18-20 minutes or until softened and golden.

2 Lightly beat the eggs, thyme, sage, and ricotta together in a small bowl, season well with salt and black pepper, and then pour evenly over the butternut squash. Cook for another 2-3 minutes, until the egg mixture is almost set, stirring occasionally with a heat-resistant rubber spatula to prevent the bottom from burning.

3 Slide the pan under a preheated medium-hot broiler and broil for 3-4 minutes or until the top is set and the frittata is golden. Slice into 6 wedges and serve hot.

1 tablespoon canola oil
1 red onion, thinly sliced
½ butternut squash, seeded peeled, and diced
8 eggs
1 tablespoon chopped thyme
2 tablespoons chopped sage
½ cup ricotta cheese
salt and black pepper

Serves **6**
Prep time **10 minutes**
Cooking time **25-30 minutes**

BRAIN FOOD

You'll need all the brain capacity you can get while you're studying, so make sure your diet includes foods that can help you reach your maximum potential. Certain foods contain essential nutrients that will help you concentrate and focus when you're studying, and they will help to naturally calm your nerves and stop you stressing out before exams.

BRIGHT MEAL IDEAS

BREAKFAST

Yogurt The probiotics in "live" yogurt, along with the calcium, make it the perfect choice for the first meal of the day. Spoon it over your granola or cereal and top with a drizzle of honey.

Yeast extract Love it or loathe it, with its vitamin B and iron content, a yeast extract, such as Marmite, should be the spread of choice for your morning toast.

LUNCH

Whole-grain bread Slow-release carbohydrates are needed at lunchtime to keep you feeling full and able to concentrate throughout the afternoon.

Eggs Protein should be present at every meal and if you combine your whole-grain bread with an egg filling, you've got it covered. Eggs could help to improve your cognitive skills, which makes them the perfect student food.

DINNER

Salmon Omega-3-rich salmon is the ideal choice for a healthy dinner, because it can contribute to healthy brain function. Choose fresh salmon steaks or fillets, or try adding smoked salmon to pasta dishes.

Broccoli Team your salmon with a pile of steamed broccoli and you'll be the brightest student in the classroom.

BRAINY SNACKS

Nuts and seeds These handy snacks are a really good source of vitamin E.

Bananas With potassium and serotonin-producing tryptophan, they provide the ideal snack for focusing on the task in hand. Bananas are also believed to aid sleep, so if you need to wind down after studying, peel and eat one before bedtime.

Dark chocolate If you need an excuse to nibble on a square or two of dark chocolate, then remind yourself that it can aid blood flow to the brain ... and keep nibbling.

SUPERFOODS

There's much debate about whether certain foods should be singled out for being "superfoods." But there's no denying that these ingredients could give you a boost in the brain cell department.

Pumpkin seeds

Blueberries

Green tea

Leafy green vegetables

Avocado

Tomatoes

Garlic

Beet

KEDGEREE-STYLE RICE WITH SPINACH

1 Place the haddock and peas in a skillet, cover with the boiling water, and bring to a boil. Reduce the heat, cover, and simmer for 3-4 minutes, adding the spinach for the final minute of cooking.

2 Meanwhile, prepare the instant rice according to the package directions. Drain the fish, spinach, and peas and flake the fish. Return to the pan and add the butter, garam masala, and rice, season with black pepper, and toss well. Serve sprinkled with parsley, if desired.

8 oz smoked haddock fillets, such as Finnan Haddie, or other smoked fish fillets
1 cup frozen peas
2/3 cup boiling water
8 cups spinach leaves
4 cups instant rice
2 tablespoons butter
1/2 teaspoon garam masala
black pepper
3 tablespoons chopped parsley, to garnish (optional)

Serves **4**
Prep time **5 minutes**
Cooking time **5 minutes**

AFFORDABILITY
2

BARLEY & GINGER RISOTTO
WITH BUTTERNUT SQUASH

1 Cut the squash into ¾ inch cubes, discarding the skin and any seeds. Put in an ovenproof casserole with the onion and oil and stir to mix. Bake, covered, in a preheated oven 350°F, for 30 minutes.

2 Stir in the garlic, pearl barley, rosemary, ginger and broth. Return to the oven, uncovered, and bake for another 50 minutes. Stir the risotto occasionally during cooking until the barley is tender, adding a little more water if the consistency runs dry.

3 Remove the rosemary stems. Season the risotto with plenty of black pepper and stir in the sour cream. Spoon into bowls and serve sprinkled with cheese, if desired.

½ large butternut squash
1 onion, chopped
1 tablespoon olive or sunflower oil
2 garlic cloves, thinly sliced
¾ cup pearl barley
2 large sprigs of rosemary
1 inch piece of fresh root ginger,
  peeled and finely chopped
1¼ cups Vegetable Broth
  (see page 244)
¼ cup reduced-fat sour cream
black pepper
grated Parmesan-style cheese,
  to serve (optional)

Serves **2**
Prep time **15 minutes**
Cooking time **1 hour 20 minutes**

LEMON & HERB RISOTTO (V)

1. Heat the oil in a heavy saucepan, add the shallots, garlic, celery, zucchini, and carrot, and sauté gently for 4 minutes or until the vegetables have softened. Add the rice and turn up the heat. Stir-fry for 2–3 minutes.

2. Add a ladleful of hot broth followed by half of the herbs, then season well with salt and black pepper. Reduce the heat to medium-low and add the remaining broth, 1 ladleful at a time, stirring constantly until each amount is absorbed and the rice is just firm to the bite but cooked through.

3. Remove from the heat and gently stir in the remaining herbs, the butter, lemon zest, and cheese. Place the lid on the pan and let sit for 2–3 minutes, during which time it will become creamy and oozy. Serve immediately, sprinkled with black pepper.

1 tablespoon olive oil
3 shallots, finely chopped
2 cloves garlic, finely chopped
1 head of celery, finely chopped
1 zucchini, finely diced
1 carrot, finely diced
1½ cups risotto rice
5 cups hot Vegetable Broth (see page 244)
good handful of fresh mixed herbs, such as tarragon, parsley, chives, and dill
1 stick (4 oz) butter
1 tablespoon finely grated lemon zest
1¼ cups grated Parmesan-style cheese
salt and black pepper

Serves **4**
Prep time **10 minutes**
Cooking time **30 minutes, plus standing**

AFFORDABILITY
2

MIXED BEAN & TOMATO
CHILI Ⓥ

1. Heat the oil in a heavy saucepan and add the onion and garlic. Stir-fry for 3–4 minutes, then add the dried red pepper flakes, cumin, and cinnamon.

2. Stir-fry for 2–3 minutes, then stir in the tomatoes. Bring to a boil, reduce the heat to medium, and simmer gently for 10 minutes.

3. Stir in all the beans (and chili sauce) and cook for 3–4 minutes, until warmed through. Season well with salt and black pepper and ladle into 4 bowls to serve.

4. Top each serving with a tablespoon of sour cream, garnish with chopped cilantro, and serve immediately with corn tortillas.

2 tablespoons olive oil
1 onion, finely chopped
4 garlic cloves, crushed
1 teaspoon dried red pepper flakes
2 teaspoons ground cumin
1 teaspoon ground cinnamon
1 (14½ oz) can diced tomatoes
2 cups rinsed and drained mixed canned beans, such as kidney beans, pinto beans, and chickpeas (garbanzo beans)
1 (15 oz) can red kidney beans in chili sauce
salt and black pepper

To serve
¼ cup reduced-fat sour cream
⅓ cup finely chopped fresh cilantro, to garnish
warm corn tortillas

Serves **4**
Prep time **10 minutes**
Cooking time **25 minutes**

AFFORDABILITY
1

CAULIFLOWER WITH CHICKPEAS (V)

1 Heat the oil in a large, nonstick skillet over medium heat. Add the scallions and stir-fry for 2-3 minutes. Add the garlic, ginger, and curry powder and stir-fry for 20-30 seconds until fragrant. Add the cauliflower and bell peppers and stir-fry for another 2-3 minutes.

2 Stir in the tomatoes and bring to a boil. Cover, reduce the heat a little, and simmer for 10 minutes, stirring occasionally. Add the chickpeas, season to taste with salt and black pepper, and bring back to a boil.

3 Remove from the heat and serve immediately with steamed rice and a mint and cucumber yogurt relish, if desired.

VARIATION
For broccoli with black-eyed peas, follow the recipe above, replacing the cauliflower with 4 cups broccoli florets and the chickpeas with 1 (15 oz) can black-eyed peas.

1 tablespoon peanut oil
8 scallions, cut into 2 inch lengths
2 teaspoons grated garlic
2 teaspoons ground ginger
2 tablespoons medium curry powder
2 cups cauliflower florets
1 red bell pepper, cored, seeded, and diced
1 yellow bell pepper, cored, seeded, and diced
1 (14½ oz) can diced tomatoes
1 (15 oz) can chickpeas (garbanzo beans), rinsed and drained
salt and black pepper

To serve
Boiled Rice (see page 247) (optional)
mint and cucumber yogurt relish (riata; optional)

Serves **4**
Prep time **10 minutes**
Cooking time **20 minutes**

VEGETABLE CURRY WITH RICE

AFFORDABILITY 1

V

1 Heat the oil in a large skillet and cook the onion and mixed vegetables over medium heat for about 10 minutes, stirring frequently, until lightly browned and beginning to soften. Stir in the garlic and ginger and cook for another 2 minutes, then add the curry paste and stir over the heat for 1 minute to cook the spices.

2 Pour in the diced tomatoes and broth, then bring to a boil, reduce the heat, and simmer gently for about 15 minutes, stirring occasionally, until the curry has thickened slightly and the vegetables are tender. Serve spooned over boiled rice.

2 tablespoons vegetable oil
1 onion, coarsely chopped
4 cups mixed chopped vegetables, such as carrots, leeks, sweet potato, potato, cauliflower, and broccoli
2 garlic cloves, chopped
1 inch piece of fresh ginger root, peeled and chopped
¼ cup medium-hot curry paste, such as rogan josh
1 (14 ½ oz) can diced tomatoes
1⅔ cups Vegetable Broth (see page 244)
Boiled Rice (see page 247), to serve

Serves **4**
Prep time **10 minutes**
Cooking time **30 minutes**

Vegetable, Fruit & Nut
BIRYANI Ⓥ

1 Bring a large saucepan of lightly salted water to a boil and cook the rice for 5 minutes. Add the cauliflower and cook with the rice for another 10 minutes or until both are tender (you may need to adjust the timing for the rice according to the package directions), then drain.

2 Meanwhile, heat the oil in a large, heavy skillet and cook the sweet potatoes and onion over medium heat, stirring occasionally, for 10 minutes, until browned and tender. Add the curry paste, turmeric, and mustard seeds and cook, stirring, for another 2 minutes.

3 Pour in the broth and add the green beans. Bring to a boil, then reduce the heat and simmer for 5 minutes. Stir in the drained rice and cauliflower, the golden raisins, cilantro, and cashew nuts and simmer for another 2 minutes. Spoon onto serving plates and serve with poppadums or other flatbreads and the mint and cucumber yogurt relish.

1⅓ cups basmati or other
    long-grain rice
½ cauliflower, broken into florets
2 tablespoons vegetable oil
2 large sweet potatoes, peeled
    and cut into cubes
1 large onion, sliced
3 tablespoons hot curry paste
½ teaspoon ground turmeric
2 teaspoons mustard seeds
1¼ cups Vegetable Broth
    (see page 244)
2½ cups halved, trimmed
    fine green beans
⅔ cup golden raisins
⅓ cup chopped fresh cilantro
⅓ cup cashew nuts, lightly toasted
salt

To serve
poppadums or other flatbreads
mint and cucumber yogurt relish
    (riata)

Serves **4**
Prep time **10 minutes**
Cooking time **25 minutes**

AFFORDABILITY 1

BAKED
SWEET POTATOES (V)

1   Put the potatoes on a baking sheet and roast in a preheated oven, at 425°F, for 45-50 minutes, until cooked through.

2   Combine the sour cream, scallions, chives, and salt and black pepper in a bowl.

3   Cut the baked potatoes in half lengthwise, top with the butter, and spoon the sour cream mixture on top. Serve immediately.

4 sweet potatoes, scrubbed
1 cup reduced-fat sour cream
2 scallions, finely chopped
1 tablespoon snipped chives
4 tablespoons butter
salt and black pepper

Serves **4**
Prep time **5 minutes**
Cooking time **45-50 minutes**

Caribbean Chicken
WITH RICE & PEAS

1 Mix together the jerk seasoning, ginger, and lime juice in a nonmetallic bowl. Cut a few slashes across each chicken breast and coat in the mixture. Heat 2 tablespoons of the oil in a skillet, add the chicken, and cook over medium heat for 15–20 minutes, turning occasionally, until cooked through and no signs of pink when cut into with a knife.

2 Meanwhile, heat the remaining oil in a saucepan, add the onion and garlic, and sauté for 2 minutes, until slightly softened. Add the rice, broth, and coconut milk and bring to a boil, then reduce the heat, cover, and simmer for 15–20 minutes, until the liquid has been absorbed and the rice is tender, adding the kidney beans, corn, and thyme sprigs for the final 5 minutes.

3 Slice the chicken and serve with the rice mixture and lime wedges, garnished with a few sprigs of thyme.

2 teaspoons jerk seasoning
1 teaspoon peeled and grated fresh ginger root
juice of 1 lime
2 boneless, skinless chicken breasts, about 5 oz each
3 tablespoons vegetable oil
1 small onion, chopped
1 garlic clove, crushed
1 cup long-grain rice
¾ cup Chicken Broth (see page 244)
¾ cup coconut milk
1 cup rinsed and drained canned red kidney beans
⅓ cup frozen or canned corn kernels
few thyme sprigs, plus extra to garnish
lime wedges, to serve

Serves **2**
Prep time **10 minutes**
Cooking time **25 minutes**

AFFORDABILITY
2

LENTIL & CHICKEN STEW

1   Heat the oil in a medium, heavy skillet and cook the chicken and celery for 5 minutes. Add the fresh tomatoes and stir for 1 minute.

2   Add the lentils, canned tomatoes, bouillon cube, and water. Bring to a boil and boil for 2 minutes, stirring occasionally.

3   Stir in the chopped parsley, then ladle into serving bowls and serve with crusty bread to mop up the juices, if desired.

VARIATION
For a thick red lentil and chicken stew, heat 1 tablespoon olive oil and cook 2 (5 oz) thinly sliced chicken breasts, 1 thinly sliced large onion, and 4 chopped celery sticks over medium-high heat for 5 minutes. Add 4 coarsely chopped tomatoes, 1¼ cups red lentils, 1 (14½ oz) can diced tomatoes, and 2½ cups Chicken Broth (see page 244). Bring to a boil, then reduce the heat, cover, and simmer, stirring occasionally, for 20 minutes or until the lentils are soft and tender. Season to taste with salt and black pepper and stir in ⅓ cup chopped parsley. Serve with warm crusty bread.

1 tablespoon olive oil
2 chicken breasts, about 5 oz each, thinly sliced
3 celery sticks, coarsely chopped
4 tomatoes, coarsely chopped
1¼ cups cooked green lentils
1 (14½ oz) can diced tomatoes
1 chicken bouillon cube, crumbled
⅔ cup boiling water
2 tablespoons chopped parsley
crusty bread, to serve (optional)

Serves **4**
Prep time **10 minutes**
Cooking time **10 minutes**

French-Style CHICKEN STEW

AFFORDABILITY 2

1 Put the leek, chicken, potatoe,s and carrot into a large saucepan. Pour in the broth and wine and season to taste with salt and black pepper. Bring to a boil, then reduce the heat and simmer for 15 minutes, stirring occasionally, until just cooked through.

2 Stir in the peas and sour cream and heat through. Sprinkle with the tarragon and serve immediately.

VARIATION
For a chicken sauté with peas, lettuce, and tarragon, heat 1 tablespoon oil in a saucepan. Add 10 oz thinly sliced chicken breasts and cook for 2 minutes, until golden. Add 1 crushed garlic clove and cook for another 30 seconds. Pour in ¼ cup dry white wine and simmer for 1 minute, then add ¼ cup Chicken Broth (see page 244) and boil hard for 2 minutes. Stir in ⅔ cup defrosted frozen peas, 1 sliced Boston, Bibb, or other small butterhead lettuce, and 2 tablespoons sour cream, season to taste with salt and black pepper, and heat through. Sprinkle with chopped tarragon and serve with lightly toasted French bread slices.

1 leek, trimmed, cleaned, and sliced
4 boneless, skinless chicken thighs, cut into chunks
13 oz small new potatoes, halved
1 carrot, sliced
1⅔ cups Chicken Broth (see page 244)
¼ cup dry white wine
⅔ cup frozen peas, defrosted
2 tablespoons reduced-fat sour cream
salt and black pepper
handful of chopped tarragon, to garnish

Serves **4**
Prep time **10 minutes**
Cooking time **20 minutes**

CHICKEN & SPINACH STEW

1 Mix the chicken with the ground spices until well coated. Heat the oil in a large saucepan, Dutch oven, or flameproof casserole, then add the chicken and cook for 2-3 minutes, until lightly browned.

2 Stir in the tomato paste, tomatoes, raisins, cooked lentils, and lemon zest, season with salt and black pepper, and simmer gently, stirring occasionally, for about 12 minutes, until thickened slightly and the chicken is cooked.

3 Add the spinach and stir until wilted. Ladle the stew into serving bowls, then sprinkle with the parsley and serve with steamed couscous or rice.

VARIATION

For chicken and rice soup with lemon, heat 2 tablespoons olive oil in a large saucepan and cook 4 sliced scallions and 2 chopped garlic cloves over medium heat for 2-3 minutes to soften. Add 7 oz thinly sliced, boneless, skinless chicken breasts and cook for 3-4 minutes, until lightly browned all over. Add 1 cup long-grain rice and stir to coat in the oil. Pour 5 cups Chicken or Vegetable Broth (see pages 244) into the pan, season to taste with salt and black pepper, add a pinch of freshly grated nutmeg, then simmer, covered, for about 15 minutes, until the rice is tender. Stir 5 cups mixed chopped watercress and spinach leaves into the soup and stir for 1-2 minutes, until the leaves have wilted. Ladle into bowls and serve with lemon wedges.

1¼ lb boneless, skinless chicken thighs, thinly sliced
2 teaspoons ground cumin
1 teaspoon ground ginger
2 tablespoons olive oil
1 tablespoon tomato paste
2 (14½ oz) cans cherry tomatoes
⅔ cup raisins
1¼ cups cooked green lentils
1 teaspoon finely grated lemon zest
5 cups baby spinach
salt and black pepper
handful of chopped parsley, to garnish
steamed couscous or Boiled Rice (see page 247), to serve

Serves **4**
Prep time **10 minutes**
Cooking time **20 minutes**

CHICKEN
JALFREZI

1   Heat the oil in a large skillet, add the chicken, onion, and green bell pepper, and cook over medium heat, stirring occasionally, for 10 minutes, until starting to turn golden. Add the chile and spices and cook for 2–3 minutes, then stir in the tomatoes and cook for another 3 minutes.

2   Stir in the yogurt, then pour in the water, cover, and simmer gently for 10 minutes, until the chicken is cooked through and the flavors have infused, stirring occasionally and adding a little more water, if necessary. Serve with warm naan to mop up the juices.

2 tablespoons sunflower oil
10 oz boneless, skinless chicken
   breasts, cut into pieces
1 onion, cut into thin wedges
1 small green bell pepper, cored,
   seeded, and cut into chunks
1 green chile, seeded and finely
   chopped
1 teaspoon ground cumin
1 teaspoon garam masala
½ teaspoon ground turmeric
2 tomatoes, cut into wedges
2 tablespoons plain yogurt
1 cup hot water
warm naan or other flatbread,
   to serve

Serves **2**
Prep time **15 minutes**
Cooking time **30 minutes**

AFFORDABILITY
1

CHICKEN SHAWARMA

1 Heat the oil in a small skillet and sauté the onion for 3 minutes, until softened. Add the chicken and cook for another 5 minutes, stirring frequently until the chicken is cooked through. Stir in the shawarma spice and cook for another 1 minute.

2 Lightly toast the pita bread. Mix the tahini with the honey, vinegar, and hot water in a small bowl. Season lightly with salt and black pepper.

3 Shred the lettuce on a serving plate and pile the chicken mixture on top. Sprinkle with the pickle and spoon the tahini dressing on top. Serve with the toasted pita bread.

1 teaspoon olive or vegetable oil
½ onion, thinly sliced
7 oz boneless, skinless chicken thighs, cut into large pieces
1 teaspoon shawarma spice
1 whole wheat pita bread
1 tablespoon tahini
1 teaspoon honey
1 teaspoon white or red wine vinegar
4 teaspoons hot water
1 Bibb, Boston, or other small butterhead lettuce
1 pickle, sliced
salt and black pepper

Serves **1**
Prep time **10 minutes**
Cooking time **10 minutes**

AFFORDABILITY
1

JAMBALAYA
WITH CHORIZO & PEPPERS

1 Cook the rice in a large saucepan of boiling water for about 25 minutes, or according to the package directions, until tender. Drain.

2 Meanwhile, heat the oil in a skillet and gently sauté the onion, bell peppers, and chorizo for 10-15 minutes, stirring occasionally, until softened and beginning to brown.

3 Stir in the tomatoes, allspice, and sugar and cook for 5 minutes, until the tomato juices are reduced. Stir in the cooked rice and peas and season to taste with salt and black pepper. Heat through for 5 minutes, then serve.

1 cup brown basmati or other long-grain rice
1 tablespoon olive oil
1 onion, chopped
1 red bell pepper, cored, seeded, and chopped
1 yellow bell pepper, cored, seeded, and chopped
5 oz spicy chorizo sausage, diced
1 (14½ oz) can diced tomatoes
¼ teaspoon ground allspice
1 teaspoon granulated sugar
⅔ cup frozen peas
salt and black pepper

Serves **3**
Prep time **15 minutes**
Cooking time **30 minutes**

HEALTHY TIP

ADHERE TO THE DATES Food poisoning is a daily danger for students preparing food in less than salubrious surroundings. Lower your chances by following the advice on food labels—if it has reached its expiration or use-by date, don't let it fester in the refrigerator for another couple of nights.

AFFORDABILITY
1

Chicken Burgers
WITH TOMATO SALSA

1 Mix together all the burger ingredients, except the oil. Divide the mixture into 4 and form each portion into a patty. Cover and chill for 30 minutes.

2 Combine all the salsa ingredients in a bowl. Cover and set aside.

3 Brush the patties with the oil and cook under a preheated high broiler or on a preheated barbecue grill for 3–4 minutes each side until cooked through. Serve each burger in a bread roll with the tomato salsa and some salad greens.

VARIATION

For chile and cilantro chicken burgers with mango salsa, make the burgers as above, replacing the sun-dried tomatoes with a finely chopped seeded red chile (and using cilantro pesto in place of the standard pesto). Serve with a salsa made from 1 peeled and pitted large ripe mango, 1 small red onion, and 1 seeded red chile, all finely chopped, then mixed with 2 tablespoons chopped fresh cilantro, 2 tablespoons chopped mint leaves, juice of 1 lime, and 2 teaspoons olive oil.

1 garlic clove, crushed
3 scallions, thinly sliced
1 tablespoon Pesto (see page 248)
2 tablespoons chopped mixed
  herbs, such as parsley, tarragon,
  and thyme
12 oz ground chicken
2 sun-dried tomatoes, finely
  chopped
1 teaspoon olive oil

Tomato salsa
1²⁄₃ cups quartered cherry
  tomatoes
1 red chile, seeded and finely
  chopped
1 tablespoon chopped fresh cilantro
finely grated zest and juice of 1 lime

To serve
4 bread rolls
salad greens

Serves **4**
Prep time **15 minutes,
plus chilling**
Cooking time **10 minutes**

AFFORDABILITY

CHICKEN FAJITAS
WITH NO-CHILE SALSA

1 To make the chicken fajitas, put all the ground spices, garlic, and chopped cilantro into a mixing bowl. Cut the chicken into bite-size strips and toss in the oil, then add to the spices and toss to coat lightly in the spice mixture.

2 Make the salsa. Mix the tomatoes, cilantro, and cucumber in a bowl and drizzle with the oil. Transfer to a serving bowl.

3 Make the guacamole. Mash the avocado in a bowl with the lime zest and juice and sweet chili sauce, if using, until soft and having a rough texture.

4 Heat a ridged grill pan or heavy skillet until hot and cook the chicken for 3–4 minutes, turning occasionally, until golden and cooked through. Top the tortillas with the hot chicken strips, guacamole, and salsa, and fold into quarters to serve.

VARIATION
For sour cream chicken tacos, cook the chicken as above and spoon into 8 warm, prepared taco shells. Serve 2 per person with 1½ teaspoons reduced-fat sour cream and some fresh cilantro leaves on each.

½ teaspoon ground coriander
½ teaspoon ground cumin
½ teaspoon paprika
1 garlic clove, crushed
3 tablespoons chopped fresh cilantro
12 oz boneless, skinless chicken breasts
1 tablespoon olive oil
4 soft flour tortillas

Salsa
3 ripe tomatoes, finely chopped
3 tablespoons chopped fresh cilantro
⅛ cucumber, finely chopped
1 tablespoon olive oil

Guacamole
1 large ripe avocado, peeled, pitted, and chopped
finely grated zest and juice of ½ lime
sweet chili sauce, to taste (optional)

Serves **4**
Prep time **20 minutes**
Cooking time **5 minutes**

AFFORDABILITY
2

POT ROAST CHICKEN

THIS DISH MAKES A DELIGHTFUL CHANGE FROM A TRADITIONAL ROASTED CHICKEN. IF YOU HAVE ANY LEFTOVER CHICKEN, MIX WITH MAYO AND SHREDDED LETTUCE FOR AN EASY SANDWICH FILLING.

1 Season the chicken all over with salt and black pepper. Melt the butter with the oil in a skillet and cook the chicken on all sides. Transfer to a large Dutch oven or ovenproof casserole.

2 Sauté the sliced onion and celery in the pan juices for 6-8 minutes or until browned. Stir in the garlic, wine, and herbs and pour the mixture over the chicken. Cover and bake in a preheated oven, at 325°F, for 1 hour.

3 Meanwhile, rinse the lentils and put them into a saucepan with plenty of water. Bring to a boil and boil for 10 minutes. Drain well.

4 Spread the lentils around the chicken and return to the oven for another 45 minutes. Transfer the cooked chicken and lentil mixture to a warmed serving dish and cover. Remember to remove the bay leaves and thyme stems before serving.

5 Mix the capers, parsley, and sour cream together in a small saucepan and heat through gently, stirring. Serve with the carved chicken and the lentil mixture.

1 (3 lb) oven-ready chicken
2 tablespoons butter
2 tablespoons olive oil
1 onion, sliced
3 celery sticks, sliced
4-6 garlic cloves, crushed
1 cup dry white wine
3 bay leaves
sprigs of thyme
3/4 cup green lentils
2 tablespoons capers, drained
1/4 cup chopped parsley
1/2 cup reduced-fat sour cream
salt and black pepper

Serves **4**
Prep time **15 minutes**
Cooking time **2 hours**

ROASTED LEMONY CHICKEN WITH ZUCCHINI

1. Cut a few slashes across each chicken thigh. Mix together the lemon zest, crushed garlic, and 2 tablespoons of the oil in a bowl, then rub this mixture over the chicken thighs, pushing it into the slashes.

2. Place the chicken in a roasting pan with the potatoes and season with salt and black pepper. Roast in a preheated oven, at 425°F, for 10 minutes.

3. Add the onion, zucchini, unpeeled garlic cloves, and thyme leaves to the pan and drizzle with the remaining oil. Return to the oven and roast for another 15 minutes or until the chicken is golden and cooked through and the vegetables are tender.

4. Squeeze the soft garlic over the chicken and vegetables, discarding the skin, and serve garnished with thyme sprigs.

4 chicken thighs, about 4 oz each
finely grated zest of 1 lemon
1 garlic clove, crushed, plus
   2 whole cloves, unpeeled
¼ cup olive oil
12 oz new potatoes, halved if large
1 red onion, cut into wedges
1 zucchini, thickly sliced
1 tablespoon thyme leaves, plus
   a few sprigs to garnish
salt and black pepper

Serves **2**
Prep time **10 minutes**
Cooking time **25 minutes**

AFFORDABILITY
1

WARM CHICKEN, MED VEG & BULGUR WHEAT SALAD

1 Heat 1/3 cup of the oil in a large skillet, add the zucchini, onion, red bell pepper, eggplant, and garlic, and cook over high heat for 15-20 minutes, stirring regularly, until golden and softened.

2 Meanwhile, cook the bulgur wheat in a saucepan of lightly salted boiling water for 15 minutes, or according to the package directions, until tender.

3 While the bulgur wheat is cooking, brush the remaining 1 tablespoon of oil over the chicken breasts and season well with salt and black pepper. Heat a large ridged grill pan or skillet until smoking, then add the chicken and cook over high heat for 4-5 minutes on each side or until golden and cooked through. Remove from the heat and thinly slice diagonally.

4 Drain the bulgur wheat. Place in a large bowl, toss with the parsley, and season with salt and black pepper. Add the hot vegetables and chicken, toss together, and serve.

1/3 cup plus 1 tablespoon olive oil
1 large zucchini, cut into thick slices
1 large red onion, cut into thin wedges
1 red bell pepper, cored, seeded, and cut into chunks
1/2 small eggplant, cut into small chunks
1 garlic clove, thinly sliced
1 cup bulgur wheat
4 chicken breasts, about 5 oz each
1/4 cup chopped parsley
salt and black pepper

Serves **4**
Prep time **15 minutes**
Cooking time **20 minutes**

AFFORDABILITY
1

OVEN-BAKED TURKEY & GRUYÈRE BURGERS

1 Thinly slice half of the onion and reserve. Finely chop the remainder and mix in a bowl with the ground turkey, dried herbs, and a little salt and black pepper. Divide into 4 even portions. Cut the Gruyère into 4 pieces and push a piece into the center of each portion of ground turkey. Flatten out into patty shapes.

2 Brush a baking sheet with a little of the oil and place the patties on top. Brush the patties with the remaining oil, then bake in a preheated oven, at 400°F, for 20 minutes, turning the burgers halfway through cooking.

3 Halve the buns. Stir the walnuts into the mayonnaise and season with black pepper. Place the burgers on the bun bottoms and top with the walnut mayonnaise, watercress, and sliced onion. Top with the hamburger bun lids and serve.

1 small red onion
1 lb ground turkey
½ teaspoon dried thyme or oregano
3 oz piece Gruyère cheese
1 teaspoon olive or sunflower oil
2 seeded hamburger buns
¼ cup walnuts, finely chopped
¼ cup mayonnaise
½ bunch of watercress or 2 cups other peppery greens
salt and black pepper

Serves **4**
Prep time **10 minutes**
Cooking time **20 minutes**

AFFORDABILITY
3

SWEDISH MEATBALLS

COATED IN A SWEET, SPICY CRANBERRY GLAZE, THESE BITE-SIZE MEATBALLS MAKE A GOOD STUDENT DINNER SERVED WITH PAPPARDELLE OR TAGLIATELLE. MIXING THE MEAT AND FLAVORINGS IN A BLENDER OR FOOD PROCESSOR GIVES THE MEATBALLS THEIR CHARACTERISTIC SMOOTH TEXTURE.

1 Make the cranberry glaze. Combine the cranberry sauce, broth, chili sauce, and lemon juice in a small saucepan and heat gently until smooth, stirring, then simmer gently for 5 minutes. Remove from the heat and set aside.

2 Meanwhile, put the ground veal and pork into a food processor with the onion, garlic, bread crumbs, egg yolk, parsley, and a little salt and black pepper, and process until the mixture forms a smooth paste that clings together.

3 Scoop teaspoonfuls of the paste and roll them into small balls between the palms of your hands.

4 Heat the oil in a large, heavy skillet and cook half of the meatballs, turning occasionally, for 8-10 minutes, until golden. Drain and cook the remainder. Return all the meatballs to the pan and add the cranberry glaze. Cook gently for 2-3 minutes, until hot. Serve immediately.

10 oz lean ground veal or
  ground beef chuck
8 oz lean ground pork
1 small onion, chopped
1 garlic clove, crushed
1/2 cup fresh bread crumbs
1 egg yolk
3 tablespoons chopped
  flat leaf parsley
2 tablespoons vegetable oil
salt and black pepper

Cranberry glaze
1/2 cup good-quality cranberry
  sauce
1/2 cup Chicken or Vegetable Broth
  (see pages 244)
2 tablespoons sweet chili sauce
1 tablespoon lemon juice

Serves **4**
Prep time **20 minutes**
Cooking time **30 minutes**

AFFORDABILITY
2

BACON-WRAPPED MEAT LOAF

1 Spead out the red bell peppers and onion in a roasting pan and drizzle with the oil. Cook in a preheated oven, at 400°F, for 30 minutes, until lightly roasted, then remove and chop. Reduce the oven temperature to 325°F.

2 Use some bacon slices to line the bottom and long sides of a 9 x 5 x 3 inch loaf pan, overlapping them slightly and letting the ends overhang the sides. Finely chop the rest of the bacon.

3 Mix together both ground meats, the chopped bacon, roasted vegetables, herbs, Worcestershire sauce, tomato paste, bread crumbs, egg, and salt and black pepper.

4 Pack the mixture evenly into the pan and fold the ends of the bacon over the filling. Cover with aluminum foil, place in a roasting pan, and pour in ¾ inch boiling water. Cook in the oven for 2 hours or until cooked through.

5 To serve hot, remove from the oven and let the meat loaf rest in the pan for 15 minutes, then invert onto a serving plate. To serve cold, cool it in the pan, then remove, wrap in aluminum foil, and refrigerate before serving.

2 red bell peppers, cored, seeded, and cut into chunks
1 red onion, sliced
3 tablespoons olive oil
10 oz thin-cut bacon slices
1 lb ground round beef
8 oz ground pork
2 tablespoons chopped oregano
2 tablespoons chopped flat leaf parsley
3 tablespoons Worcestershire sauce
2 tablespoons tomato paste
1 cup fresh bread crumbs
1 egg
salt and black pepper

Serves **6**
Prep time **30 minutes, plus optional cooling**
Cooking time **2½ hours, plus standing**

AFFORDABILITY 3

ROAST PORK LOIN
WITH CREAMY CABBAGE & LEEKS

1 Mix together the spices in a bowl, then rub over the pork. Heat 1 tablespoon of the oil in a Dutch oven or ovenproof skillet, add the pork, and cook until browned on all sides. Transfer to a preheated oven, at 350°F, and cook for 20-25 minutes or until cooked through. Let rest for 2 minutes.

2 Meanwhile, cook the sweet potatoes in a saucepan of boiling water for 12-15 minutes, until tender, adding the cabbage and leeks 3-4 minutes before the end of the cooking time. Drain well.

3 Heat the remaining oil in a skillet, add the drained vegetables, and sauté for 7-8 minutes, stirring occasionally, until starting to turn golden. Stir in the sour cream and mustard.

4 Slice the pork and serve on top of the vegetables.

1 teaspoon ground cumin
1 teaspoon ground coriander
1 lb pork loin, trimmed of fat
3 tablespoons olive oil
2 sweet potatoes, peeled and chopped
2½ cups shredded savoy cabbage
3 leeks, trimmed, cleaned, and sliced
3 tablespoons reduced-fat sour cream
2 teaspoons whole-grain mustard

Serves **4**
Prep time **10 minutes**
Cooking time **30 minutes**

GARLICKY PORK
with Warm Lima Bean Salad

1 Mix together the oil and garlic in a bowl, then season with salt and black pepper. Place the pork on an aluminum foil-lined broiler rack and spoon the garlicky oil over it. Cook under a preheated medium broiler for about 10 minutes, turning occasionally, until golden and cooked through.

2 Meanwhile, make the salad. Heat the oil in a large skillet, add the lima beans and tomatoes, and heat through for a few minutes. Add the broth, lemon juice, and parsley and season with salt and black pepper. Serve with the broiled chops or cutlets.

¼ cup olive oil
2 garlic cloves, crushed
4 lean pork chops or cutlets, about 5 oz each
salt and black pepper

Salad
2 tablespoons olive oil
2 (15 oz) cans lima beans, rinsed and drained
12 cherry tomatoes, halved
⅔ cup Chicken Broth (see page 244)
juice of 2 lemons
2 handfuls of parsley, chopped

Serves **4**
Prep time **10 minutes**
Cooking time **10 minutes**

AFFORDABILITY
2

ONE-PAN SPICED PORK

AFFORDABILITY 1

THIS IS A GREAT DISH FOR NO-FUSS ENTERTAINING, WHEN YOU WANT TO IMPRESS YOUR BUDDIES. SIMPLY PUT THE PORK CHOPS INTO A ROASTING PAN WITH THE OTHER INGREDIENTS AND LET THEM BAKE, SAFE IN THE KNOWLEDGE THAT DINNER WILL LOOK AFTER ITSELF.

1 Snip through the fat on the rind of the pork chops so that they do not curl up during cooking. Put them into a large roasting pan with the parsnips, squash, and apples.

2 Crush the fennel and coriander seeds using a mortar and pestle, then mix with the garlic, turmeric, oil, and honey. Season with salt and black pepper, then brush the mixture over the pork and vegetables.

3 Cook in a preheated oven, at 375ºF, for 35–40 minutes, turning the vegetables once, until golden brown and tender. Spoon onto plates and serve.

4 loin pork chops, about 6 oz each
3 parsnips or small sweet
  potatoes, cut into chunks
1 butternut squash, peeled,
  seeded, and thickly sliced
2 sweet, crisp red-skinned apples,
  cored and quartered
1 teaspoon fennel seeds
2 teaspoon coriander seeds
2 garlic cloves, chopped
1 teaspoon ground turmeric
3 tablespoons olive oil
1 tablespoon honey
salt and black pepper

Serves **4**
Prep time **15 minutes**
Cooking time **40 minutes**

HEALTHY TIP

KEEP TABS ON YOUR ENERGY DRINKS A drink or two may help get you through a class, but it all adds up. Energy drinks may give you energy at first, but the caffeine they contain can keep you awake at night and raise blood pressure.

BAKED SPICY SAUSAGES

MAKE THIS QUICK AND EASY MEAL WITH THE MOST GARLICKY, SPICY SAUSAGES YOU CAN FIND—ITALIAN-STYLE SAUSAGES ARE AN IDEAL CHOICE. THEIR FLAVOR WILL MINGLE WITH ALL THE OTHER INGREDIENTS AS THEY COOK.

1 Slice each sausage into quarters. Heat the oil in a large, heavy skillet and gently cook the sausages and onion for about 10 minutes, until golden, gently shaking the pan frequently.

2 Add the tomatoes, oregano, and red kidney beans. Reduce the heat to its lowest setting, cover, and cook gently for 10 minutes.

3 Meanwhile, cook the pasta in a large saucepan of lightly salted boiling water for about 10 minutes, or according to the package directions, until just tender. Drain and add to the skillet. Add half of the cheese and toss the ingredients together until mixed.

4 Transfer to a 1½ quart shallow, ovenproof dish and sprinkle with the remaining cheese. Bake in a preheated oven, at 400°F, for 20-25 minutes or until the cheese is melting and golden.

1 lb Italian sausages
2 tablespoons olive oil
1 large red onion, sliced
2 (14½ oz) cans diced tomatoes
2 tablespoons chopped oregano
1 (15 oz) can red kidney beans, rinsed and drained
8 oz dried fusilli pasta
1½ cups shredded fontina cheese
salt

Serves **4**
Prep time **15 minutes**
Cooking time **45 minutes**

CHEESY PORK WITH PARSNIP PUREE

1 Season the pork with plenty of black pepper. Heat the oil in a nonstick skillet, add the pork, and cook for 2 minutes on each side, until browned, then transfer the meat to an ovenproof dish.

2 Mix together the cheese, sage, bread crumbs, and egg yolk. Divide the mixture into 4 and use to top each of the pork chops or cutlets, pressing down gently. Cook in a preheated oven, at 400°F, for 12-15 minutes, until the topping is golden.

3 Meanwhile, make the parsnip puree. Place the parsnips and garlic in a saucepan of boiling water and cook for 10-12 minutes, until tender. Drain, then mash with the sour cream and plenty of black pepper. Serve with the pork and steamed green beans or cabbage.

VARIATION
For chicken with breaded tomato topping, replace the pork with 4 boneless, skinless chicken breasts. Brown and lay in an ovenproof dish, as above. Make the topping as above, replacing the sage with 4 chopped sun-dried tomatoes and ¼ teaspoon dried oregano. Bake as above and serve with the parsnip puree.

4 lean pork chops or cutlets, about 4 oz each
1 teaspoon olive oil
½ cup crumbled cheese, such as Wensleydale, or shredded cheddar cheese
1½ teaspoons chopped sage
1½ cups fresh whole-grain bread crumbs
1 egg yolk, beaten
black pepper

Parsnip puree
5 parsnips (about 1¼ lb), chopped
2 garlic cloves, peeled
3 tablespoons reduced-fat sour cream
steamed green beans or cabbage, to serve

Serves **4**
Prep time **10 minutes**
Cooking time **20 minutes**

Chorizo & HAM EGGS

1 Heat the oil in a skillet, add the red bell pepper and chorizo, and cook over high heat for 2 minutes, until golden. Add the tomatoes and cook for another 2 minutes, then add the sliced ham and spinach and cook, stirring occasionally, for 2 minutes.

2 Divide the mixture between 2 small, individual pans, if you have them (if not, continue to cook in one pan). Make wells in the tomato mixture and break an egg into each well. Cover and cook over medium heat for 2-3 minutes, until set. Serve with warm crusty bread to mop up the juices.

1 tablespoon olive oil
1 small red bell pepper, cored, seeded, and sliced
4 oz chorizo sausage, thinly sliced
2 tomatoes, coarsely chopped
2 oz wafer-thin ham slices
2 handfuls of baby spinach leaves
2 extra-large eggs
warm crusty bread, to serve

Serves **2**
Prep time **5 minutes**
Cooking time **10 minutes**

AFFORDABILITY
1

LIMA BEAN & CHORIZO STEW

1 Heat the oil in a flameproof casserole, add the onion and garlic, and sauté for 1-2 minutes. Stir in the chorizo and cook until beginning to brown. Add the bell peppers and sauté for 3 minutes.

2 Pour in the wine and let it reach a simmer, then stir in the lima beans, tomatoes, and tomato paste and season well with salt and black pepper. Cover and simmer for 15 minutes, stirring occasionally.

3 Ladle into shallow bowls, sprinkle with the parsley to garnish, and serve with crusty bread, if desired.

VARIATION
For garlic shrimp with lima beans, cook the onion and garlic as above, then stir in 10 oz peeled and deveined, raw jumbo shrimp instead of the chorizo and cook until they just turn pink. Add the lima beans, 3 tablespoons reduced-fat sour cream, and 2 handfuls of arugula and season well with salt and black pepper. Heat through and serve.

1 tablespoon olive oil
1 large onion, chopped
2 garlic cloves, crushed
7 oz chorizo sausage, sliced
1 green bell pepper, cored, seeded, and chopped
1 red bell pepper, cored, seeded, and chopped
1 small glass of red wine
2 (15 oz) cans lima beans, rinsed and drained
1 (14½ oz) can cherry tomatoes
1 tablespoon tomato paste
salt and black pepper
chopped parsley, to garnish
crusty bread, to serve (optional)

Serves **4**
Prep time **10 minutes**
Cooking time **20 minutes**

WEST INDIAN
Beef & Bean Stew

1 Heat the oil in a large, heavy saucepan, add the beef and cook, stirring, over medium-high heat for 5-6 minutes or until browned. Add the cloves, onion, and curry powder and cook for 2-3 minutes, until the onion is beginning to soften, then stir in the carrots, celery, thyme, garlic, and tomato paste.

2 Pour in the broth and stir well, then add the potato and beans and bring to a boil. Reduce the heat slightly and simmer for 20 minutes, uncovered, stirring occasionally, until the potatoes and beef are tender. Season to taste with salt and black pepper. Ladle into bowls and serve with lemon wedges.

3 tablespoons sunflower oil
1¾ lb ground round beef
6 whole cloves
1 onion, finely chopped
2 tablespoons medium curry powder
2 carrots, cut into ½ inch cubes
2 celery sticks, diced
1 tablespoon thyme leaves
2 garlic cloves, crushed
¼ cup tomato paste
2½ cups beef broth
1 large Yukon gold or white round potato, peeled and cut into ½ inch cubes
¾ cup rinsed and drained canned black beans
¾ cup rinsed and drained canned black-eyed peas
salt and black pepper
lemon wedges, to serve

Serves **4-6**
Prep time **10 minutes**
Cooking time **30 minutes**

AFFORDABILITY 2

BEEF, SQUASH & PRUNE STEW

1 Heat the oil in a large saucepan or flameproof casserole, add the garlic, onion, squash, and steak, and cook over high heat for 5-10 minutes, stirring occasionally, until the beef is browned and the squash is golden. Add the spices and cook for another 1 minute.

2 Add the prunes, tomatoes, and broth and bring to a boil, then reduce the heat, cover, and simmer for 15 minutes, stirring occasionally, until the stew is thickened and the meat and vegetables are cooked through.

3 Sprinkle with the chopped cilantro and stir through. Serve with steamed couscous, if desired, topped with spoonfuls of yogurt.

2 tablespoons olive oil
1 garlic clove, chopped
1 large onion, chopped
3½ cups peeled, seeded, and diced butternut squash, pumpkin, or other winter squash
1¼ lb sirloin steak, diced
2 teaspoons ground coriander
2 teaspoons ground cumin
1 cup pitted dried prunes
2 (14½ oz) cans diced tomatoes
2 cups beef broth
2½ cups chopped fresh cilantro leaves

To serve
steamed couscous (optional)
plain yogurt

Serves **4**
Prep time **15 minutes**
Cooking time **25-30 minutes**

BAKED COD
WITH TOMATOES & OLIVES

1. Combine the tomatoes, olives, capers, and thyme sprigs in a roasting pan. Nestle the cod fillets in the pan, drizzle with the oil and balsamic vinegar, and season to taste with salt and black pepper. Bake in a preheated oven, at 400°F, for 15 minutes, until the fish is cooked through.

2. Transfer the fish, tomatoes, and olives to plates. Spoon the pan juices over the fish. Garnish with thyme sprigs and serve immediately with a mixed green salad, if desired.

VARIATION

For steamed cod with lemon, arrange a cod fillet on each of four 12 inch squares of aluminum foil. Top each with ½ teaspoon finely grated lemon zest, a squeeze of lemon juice, 1 tablespoon extra virgin olive oil, and salt and black pepper to taste. Fold the edges of the foil together to form packages, transfer to a baking sheet, and cook in a preheated oven, at 400°F, for 15 minutes. Remove and let rest for 5 minutes. Open the packages and serve sprinkled with chopped parsley.

16 cherry tomatoes, halved
1 cup pitted black ripe olives
2 tablespoons capers, drained
4 thyme sprigs, plus extra to garnish
4 cod fillets, about 6 oz each
2 tablespoons extra virgin olive oil
2 tablespoons balsamic vinegar
salt and black pepper
mixed green salad, to serve (optional)

Serves **4**
Prep time **5 minutes**
Cooking time **15 minutes**

HADDOCK
WITH POACHED EGGS

1 Put the potatoes into a saucepan of boiling water and cook for 12-15 minutes, until tender. Drain, lightly crush with a fork, then stir through the scallions, sour cream, and watercress and season well with black pepper. Keep warm.

2 Put the fish and milk into a large skillet with the bay leaf. Bring to a boil, then cover and simmer for 5-6 minutes, until the fish is cooked through. Remove from the heat and let stand while you poach the eggs.

3 Bring a saucepan of water to a boil, swirl the water with a spoon, and crack in an egg, letting the white wrap around the yolk. Simmer for 3 minutes, then remove and keep warm. Repeat with the remaining eggs.

4 Serve the drained poached haddock fillets on top of the crushed potatoes, each topped with a poached egg.

VARIATION
For a warm haddock, asparagus, and egg salad, replace the new potatoes with 12 oz asparagus and cook in boiling water for 5 minutes, then drain. Place in a bowl with the scallions, sour cream, and watercress, adding the leaves of a Bibb, Boston, or other small butterhead lettuce and 1 tablespoon extra virgin olive oil; toss to mix. Poach the haddock as above, remove from the milk with a slotted spoon, and break into flakes. Toss the fish in the asparagus salad and divide among 4 plates. Serve with a poached egg on top, prepared as above.

1½ lb new potatoes
4 scallions, sliced
2 tablespoons reduced-fat sour cream
¾ bunch of watercress or 3 cups peppery greens
4 smoked haddock fillets, such as Finnan Haddie, or smoked salmon, about 5 oz each
⅔ cup milk
1 bay leaf
4 eggs
black pepper

Serves **4**
Prep time **10 minutes**
Cooking time **30 minutes**

SMOKED MACKEREL KEDGEREE

1 Place the eggs in a small saucepan of boiling water and cook them for 7 minutes. Drain, run under cold water, then shell them and cut into quarters.

2 Meanwhile, melt the butter in a skillet, add the smoked mackerel, rice, and curry powder, and toss together until everything is warmed through and the rice is evenly coated.

3 Stir in the lemon juice, parsley, and the quartered boiled eggs and serve immediately.

3 extra-large eggs
2 tablespoons butter
12 oz smoked mackerel, skinned and flaked
2 cups cooked basmati or other long-grain rice
1 teaspoon mild curry powder
¼ cup lemon juice
¼ cup chopped parsley

Serves **4**
Prep time **5 minutes**
Cooking time **15 minutes**

AFFORDABILITY
1

STUDENT TIP

BAG A BARGAIN If you have space in your freezer, make the most of supermarket bargains and freeze them for when the budget is straining.

SWEET GLAZED MACKEREL
WITH CRISPY KALE & NOODLES

1 Spread out the kale into a roasting pan and drizzle with 1 teaspoon of the oil. Bake in a preheated oven, at 400°F, for 6-8 minutes, until crisped.

2 Pat the mackerel dry on paper towels and cut in half. Bring a saucepan of water to a boil and cook the noodles for 2-3 minutes, or according to the package directions, until softened.

3 Meanwhile, heat the remaining oil in a small skillet and cook the mackerel, skin side up, for 2 minutes. Turn the pieces and cook for another couple of minutes, until cooked through.

4 Drain the noodles and return to the pan. Stir in the kale and transfer to a serving plate. Arrange the fish on top.

5 Add the garlic to the skillet and cook for 30 seconds. Add the lime juice, chili sauce, sugar, and water to the saucepan and heat through. Pour the sauce over the fish and serve.

2 oz kale
2 teaspoons oil
1 large mackerel fillet (skin on), about 4 oz, defrosted if frozen
2 oz whole wheat noodles
1 small garlic clove, thinly sliced
1 tablespoon lime juice
2 tablespoons sweet chili sauce
1 teaspoon light brown or granulated sugar
2 tablespoons water

Serves **1**
Prep time **5 minutes**
Cooking time **10 minutes**

ONE-PAN FISH
WITH AIOLI

1 Put the beet, potatoes, and onion into a small roasting pan with the garlic clove. Drizzle with the oil and season with a little salt and black pepper, then roast in a preheated oven at 425°F, for about 30 minutes, turning once during cooking. Add the zucchini slices to the pan and return to the oven for another 20 minutes or until the vegetables are tender and lightly roasted. Remove the garlic clove once it's soft and tender.

2 Mix the rosemary or thyme with the lemon zest and plenty of black pepper. Score the skin side of the trout with a sharp knife. Rub the herb mixture over both sides of the fish and add to the pan, skin side up. Roast for another 10-15 minutes, until the fish is cooked through.

3 Scoop out the soft pulp of the roasted garlic clove and mix it with the mayonnaise (this is aioli, or garlic mayonnaise).

4 Transfer the fish and vegetables to a serving plate, spooning over any pan juices. Serve with the aioli.

1 raw large beet, scrubbed and cut into wedges
4 oz new potatoes
1 red onion, cut into wedges
1 whole garlic clove, unpeeled
2 teaspoons olive oil
1 zucchini, sliced
½ teaspoon finely chopped rosemary or thyme
finely grated zest of ½ lemon
1 trout fillet (skin on), about 6-7 oz
2 tablespoons mayonnaise
salt and black pepper

Serves **1**
Prep time **10 minutes**
Cooking time **1 hour**

Quick Tuna
FISH CAKES

MOST OF US HAVE A COUPLE OF CANS OF TUNA IN THE PANTRY, BUT SOMETIMES THE IDEAS ABOUT WHAT TO DO WITH THEM CAN BE BORING. HERE'S A QUICK AND DELICIOUS RECIPE TO TRY—SEE IF YOU AND YOUR HOUSEMATES LIKE IT.

1 Cook the potatoes in a saucepan of lightly salted boiling water for 10 minutes or until tender. Drain well, mash, and cool slightly.

2 Flake the tuna. Beat the tuna, cheese, scallions, garlic, thyme, and egg into the mashed potatoes. Season to taste with cayenne, salt, and black pepper.

3 Divide the mixture into 4 even portions and shape each one into a thick patty. Season the flour with salt and black pepper, then dust the patties all over with the flour.

4 Heat a shallow layer of vegetable oil in a skillet until hot, then cook the fish cakes for 5 minutes on each side or until crisp and golden. Serve hot with a mixed green salad and mayonnaise.

2 russet or Yukon gold potatoes, peeled and diced
2 (5 oz) cans tuna in olive oil, drained
½ cup shredded cheddar cheese
4 scallions, finely chopped
1 small garlic clove, crushed
2 teaspoons dried thyme
1 medium egg, beaten
½ teaspoon cayenne pepper
¼ cup all-purpose flour
vegetable oil, for frying
salt and black pepper

To serve
mixed green salad
mayonnaise

Serves **4**
Prep time **15 minutes**
Cooking time **20 minutes**

AFFORDABILITY
1

RED SALMON
& ROASTED VEGETABLES

1 Mix together the eggplant, red bell peppers, onions, and garlic in a bowl with the oil and oregano and season well with salt and black pepper. Spread the vegetables out in a single layer in a nonstick roasting pan and roast in a preheated oven, at 425°F, for 25 minutes or until the vegetables are just cooked.

2 Transfer the vegetables to a warm serving dish and gently toss in the salmon and olives. Serve warm or at room temperature, garnished with basil leaves.

ACCOMPANIMENT TIP

For arugula and cucumber couscous to serve with the salmon and vegetables, put 1 cup instant couscous in a large, heatproof bowl. Season well with salt and black pepper and pour boiling hot water over the grains to just cover them. Cover and let stand for 10–12 minutes, or according to the package directions, until all the water has been absorbed. Meanwhile, finely chop 4 scallions, halve, seed, and chop ½ cucumber, and chop enough arugula so you have 3 cups prepared. Fluff up the couscous grains with a fork and transfer to a serving dish. Stir in the prepared ingredients along with 2 tablespoons olive oil and 1 tablespoon lemon juice. Toss well to mix, then serve with the salmon and vegetables.

1 eggplant, cut into bite-size pieces
2 red bell peppers, cored, seeded, and cut into bite-size pieces
2 red onions, quartered
1 garlic clove, crushed
¼ cup olive oil
pinch of dried oregano
1 (7½ oz) can red salmon, drained and flaked
1 cup pitted ripe black olives
salt and black pepper
basil leaves, to garnish

Serves **4**
Prep time **10 minutes**
Cooking time **25 minutes**

Good Grains, Beans & Legumes

ROASTED ROOTS & QUINOA SALAD

CURRIED CHICKEN
& COUSCOUS SALAD

LENTIL MOUSSAKA

SALMON &
BULGUR WHEAT PILAF

CHICKEN
WITH HERBED QUINOA & LEMON

1 Cook the quinoa in a saucepan of lightly salted boiling water for 15 minutes, or according to the package directions, until tender, then drain.

2 Meanwhile, heat the oil in a large skillet, add the onion, and sauté, stirring, for 5 minutes to soften. Add the garlic, chicken, coriander, and cumin and cook for another 8-10 minutes, stirring occasionally, until the chicken is cooked through.

3 Season the quinoa with salt and black pepper. Add the chicken mixture, cranberries, apricots, herbs, and lemon zest. Stir well and serve warm or cold.

VARIATION
For chicken and apricot Moroccan couscous, put ½ cup Moroccan-flavored couscous into a bowl, cover with boiling water, cover the bowl with plastic wrap, and let stand for 8 minutes, or according to the package directions. When all the water has been absorbed, stir in 2 cups chopped cooked chicken, 1 cup dried apricots, and 1 cup rinsed and drained, canned chickpeas.

1 cup quinoa, rinsed and drained
1 tablespoon olive oil
1 onion, chopped
1 garlic clove, crushed
4 boneless, skinless chicken
  breasts, sliced
1 teaspoon ground coriander
½ teaspoon ground cumin
⅓ cup dried cranberries
½ cup chopped dried apricots
¼ cup chopped parsley
¼ cup chopped mint
finely grated zest of 1 lemon
salt and black pepper

Serves **4**
Prep time **15 minutes**
Cooking time **15 minutes**

CHARGRILLED CHICKEN
WITH SALSA & FRUITY COUSCOUS

1 Put the chicken into a nonmetallic container, pour the vinegar over the breasts, and turn to coat. Cover and let marinate for 5 minutes.

2 Put the couscous into a heatproof bowl, pour the slightly cooled boiled water over the grains, and season with a little salt. Cover and let absorb the water for 10 minutes, or according to the package directions.

3 Meanwhile, heat 1 tablespoon of the oil in a large skillet or ridged grill pan and cook the chicken over medium heat, turning once, for 10-12 minutes, until browned and cooked through—there should be no pink when cut through with a sharp knife.

4 While the chicken is cooking, make the salsa by mixing together the avocado, tomato, 1 tablespoon of the remaining olive oil, and 1 tablespoon of the cilantro in a bowl.

5 Stir the remaining tablespoon of olive oil into the couscous, then add the raisins, pumpkin seeds, and remaining cilantro and toss again. Serve on plates topped with the chicken, with the salsa spooned over the top.

4 boneless, skinless chicken breasts, about 5 oz each
1/3 cup balsamic vinegar
1 cup couscous
1 1/2 cups boiled water, slightly cooled
3 tablespoons olive oil
1 ripe avocado, peeled, pitted, and coarsely chopped
1 large tomato, coarsely chopped
1/3 cup chopped fresh cilantro
1/3 cup raisins
1/5 cup pumpkin seeds
salt

Serves **4**
Prep time **15 minutes, plus marinating**
Cooking time **15 minutes**

Spiced Chicken
WITH MIXED GRAINS

1 Heat the oil in a saucepan and add the chicken and onion. Cook, stirring frequently for 5 minutes. Add the garlic, turmeric, dried red pepper flakes, and broth and bring to a gentle simmer. Cover and cook gently for 10 minutes.

2 Stir in the squash, wheat berries, quinoa, and mustard and cook gently for another 30 minutes, stirring occasionally, until the grains are tender and the juices are thickened. Season to taste with salt and black pepper.

3 Spoon into serving bowls and serve topped with spoonfuls of Greek yogurt.

1 tablespoon vegetable oil
1 lb boneless, skinless chicken thighs, cut into chunks
1 onion, chopped
2 garlic cloves, crushed
¼ teaspoon ground turmeric
¼ teaspoon dried red pepper flakes
2 cups Chicken or Vegetable Broth (see page 244)
2 cups peeled small butternut squash, sweet potato, or rutabaga chunks
¼ cup wheat berries
2 tablespoons quinoa, rinsed and drained
1 teaspoon whole-grain mustard
salt and black pepper
nonfat Greek yogurt, to serve

Serves **2**
Prep time **10 minutes**
Cooking time **45 minutes**

STUDENT TIP

DON'T FALL FOR CONVENIENCE If you're organized and have a weekly meal plan, you should be able to buy the majority of your grocery shopping once a week. However, if you end up wandering down to the corner or campus convenience store to stock up on staples, you'll soon feel the pinch in your pocket.

WINTER SPICED COUSCOUS

Vegan

1 Mix together the carrot, onion, and olive oil in a large, microwave-proof mug. Microwave on full power for 3 minutes, stirring after 2 minutes.

2 Stir in the spices, couscous, bouillon powder, cilantro, and chickpeas, then stir in a boiling water. Microwave on full power for another 1 minute. Stir to combine and then serve.

1 small carrot, cut into small dice
1 small red onion, chopped
2 teaspoons olive oil
good pinch each of ground allspice and ground cloves
¼ cup couscous
½ teaspoon vegetable bouillon powder
1 tablespoon chopped fresh cilantro
¼ cup rinsed and drained, canned chickpeas
¼ cup boiling water

Serves **1**
Prep time **10 minutes**
Cooking time **4 minutes**

STUDENT TIP

DON'T BE A BRAND SNOB Try swapping your staple purchases for the supermarket own-brand equivalents; you'll save a fortune and you probably won't notice the difference when it comes to taste.

AFFORDABILITY 1

Salmon
& Bulgur Wheat Pilaf

1 Cook the salmon in a steamer or microwave on full power for about 10 minutes. Alternatively, wrap it in aluminum foil and cook in a preheated oven, at 350°F, for 15 minutes.

2 Meanwhile, cook the bulgur wheat according to the package directions and cook the peas and beans in a saucepan of boiling water for about 5 minutes. Alternatively, cook the peas and beans in the steamer with the salmon.

3 Flake the salmon and mix it into the bulgur wheat with the peas and beans. Fold in the chives and parsley and season to taste with salt and black pepper. Serve immediately with the lemon wedges and yogurt.

VARIATION
For ham and bulgur wheat pilaf, lightly pan-fry 2 cups diced lean cooked ham instead of the salmon. Replace the green beans with the same quantity of shelled fava beans and fold in 2 tablespoons chopped mint along with the chives and parsley.

1 lb boneless, skinless salmon fillets
2 cups bulgur wheat
½ cup frozen peas
2 cups chopped green beans
2 tablespoons snipped chives
2 tablespoons chopped flat leaf parsley
salt and black pepper

To serve
lemon wedges
low-fat plain yogurt

Serves **4**
Prep time **10 minutes**
Cooking time **15-20 minutes**

AFFORDABILITY 2

RED KIDNEY BEAN & EGGPLANT PILAF

Vegan

1. Pour the water into a large saucepan and bring to a boil. Add the rice and turmeric and stir well to prevent the rice from sticking. Cover and simmer for 30 minutes, or according to the package directions, without stirring. Remove from the heat.

2. Meanwhile, heat the oil in a nonstick skillet, add the onion, garlic, celery, green bell pepper, and eggplant, and cook gently for 3 minutes without browning. Add the tomatoes and mushrooms, stir well, and cook for 3–4 minutes.

3. Stir the beans and the vegetable mixture into the rice, cover, and cook gently for 10 minutes.

4. Remove from the heat and let rest for 5 minutes. Stir in the parsley and season to taste with black pepper.

VARIATION
Add 4 cups chopped, cooked boneless, skinless chicken breasts before the tomatoes and mushrooms for a nonvegan meal.

2 cups water
1 cup long-grain brown rice
½ teaspoon ground turmeric
1 tablespoon vegetable oil
1 large onion, finely chopped
1 garlic clove, finely chopped
1 celery stick, finely chopped
1 green bell pepper, cored, seeded, and chopped
1 eggplant, diced
2 tomatoes, skinned and chopped
2 cups trimmed and sliced mushrooms
1 cup rinsed and drained, canned red kidney beans
2 tablespoons chopped parsley
black pepper

Serves **4**
Prep time **15 minutes**
Cooking time **40 minutes, plus resting**

HEALTHY TIP

Beans are a good source of protein, especially when they are served with a cereal food, such as rice, bread, or pasta. They are low in fat, high in fibe, and rich in many nutrients, providing iron, zinc, calcium, folate, and soluble fiber.

AFFORDABILITY 1

PASTA WITH SPICY LENTILS

THIS DISH HAS A SLIGHTLY SWEET AND SOUR FLAVOR, WHICH GIVES AN APPETIZING LIFT TO THE EARTHY FLAVOR OF THE LENTILS. YOU CAN USE ANY DRIED PASTA SHAPES WITH THIS DISH.

AFFORDABILITY 1

1 Put the lentils into a saucepan with the broth, bay leaves, and onion. Bring to a boil, reduce the heat to its lowest setting, cover, and cook gently for 20-25 minutes, or according to the package directions, until the lentils are tender and the broth has been absorbed or almost absorbed.

2 Meanwhile, bring a separate large saucepan of lightly salted water to a boil. Add the pasta, return to a boil, and cook for 8-10 minutes, or according to the package directions, until just tender.

3 While the pasta is cooking, heat 1 tablespoon of the oil in a skillet and sauté the zucchini until golden. Add the tomatoes and cook for another 1 minute to soften them slightly.

4 Beat the remaining oil with the chile, honey, mustard, and lemon juice in a small bowl.

5 Drain the pasta and return to the pan. Drain the lentils of any unabsorbed broth and add them to the pasta pan, discarding the bay leaves and onion quarters. Add the zucchini, tomatoes, dressing, and herbs and toss all the ingredients together. Check and adjust the seasoning to taste and serve warm.

1 cup black or green lentils, rinsed
4 cups Vegetable Broth
   (see page 244)
3 bay leaves
1 onion, quartered
8 oz plain or spinach-flavored
   dried pasta
1/3 cup mild olive oil
2 small zucchini, thinly sliced
16 cherry tomatoes, halved
1 red chile, thinly sliced
2 tablespoons honey
2 tablespoons whole-grain
   mustard
1 tablespoon lemon juice
1/2 cup finely chopped fresh mixed
   herbs, such as parsley, mint,
   and chives
salt and black pepper

Serves **4**
Prep time **15 minutes**
Cooking time **20-25 minutes**

TAGLIATELLE
WITH SPICY PEA FRITTERS Ⓥ

1. Put the split peas into a large bowl, cover with cold water, and let soak overnight. Drain and put in a saucepan. Cover with fresh cold water, bring to a boil, and cook for about 25 minutes, until tender. Drain.

2. Put the cooked split peas into a blender or food processor with the onion, bread crumbs, garlic, cumin, dried red pepper flakes, mint sprigs, egg, and salt and black pepper and process to a smooth paste. Divide and shape the paste firmly into small balls, each about 1 inch in diameter.

3. Bring a large saucepan of lightly salted water to a boil, add the pasta, return to a boil, and cook for about 10 minutes, until just tender.

4. Meanwhile, heat half of the oil with the butter in a large skillet. Add the pea fritters cook fry gently, stirring, for 5 minutes or until golden. You may need to cook the fritters in batches.

5. Drain the pasta and return it to the saucepan. Stir in the roasted peppers, cilantro, pea fritters, and remaining oil and mix together gently before serving.

1½ cups yellow split peas
1 onion, coarsely chopped
½ cup fresh white or whole wheat bread crumbs
2 garlic cloves, chopped
1 tablespoon crushed cumin seeds
¾ teaspoon dried red pepper flakes
several sprigs of mint
1 egg
8 oz dried tagliatelle
½ cup lemon-infused olive oil
2 tablespoons butter
1 cup drained and thinly sliced roasted red peppers in oil (from a jar)
¼ cup chopped fresh cilantro
salt and black pepper

Serves **4**
Prep time **30 minutes,
plus overnight soaking**
Cooking time **40 minutes**

SPINACH DHAL Ⓥ

NO INDIAN MEAL IS COMPLETE WITHOUT A BOWL OF SPICY LENTIL DHAL, WHICH IS ONE OF THE STAPLE DISHES EATEN THROUGHOUT THE COUNTRY. THIS ONE USES FRESH, TENDER BABY SPINACH FOR EXTRA FLAVOR, COLOR, AND TEXTURE.

1 Put the lentils into a large saucepan with the water, turmeric, and ginger. Bring to a boil. Skim off any scum that forms on the surface. Lower the heat and cook gently for 20 minutes, stirring occasionally. Stir in the spinach and chopped cilantro and cook for 8-10 minutes.

2 Heat the oil in a small, nonstick skillet until hot, then add the garlic, cumin, and mustard seeds, ground cumin, ground coriander, and red chile. Stir-fry over high heat for 2-3 minutes, then add this mixture into the lentils. Stir to mix well, season lightly with salt, then serve immediately with boiled rice or warm naan.

1¼ cups red lentils, rinsed
5 cups water
1 teaspoon ground turmeric
1 teaspoon peeled and finely grated fresh ginger root
4 cups baby spinach leaves, chopped
large handful of fresh cilantro leaves, chopped
2 teaspoons light olive oil
5 garlic cloves, thinly sliced
2 teaspoons cumin seeds
2 teaspoons mustard seeds
1 tablespoon ground cumin
1 teaspoon ground coriander
1 red chile, finely chopped
salt
Boiled Rice (see page 246) or warm naan, to serve

Serves **4**
Prep time **10 minutes**
Cooking time **35 minutes**

HEALTHY TIP

Both lentils and spinach are an excellent source of iron, making this dish a real iron-booster. Lentils are also a great source of fiber and protein, so dhal is a great choice for a vegetarian meal.

AFFORDABILITY 1

CURRIED CHICKEN COUSCOUS SALAD

1 Put the couscous into a bowl and pour over enough boiling water to just cover. Season lightly with salt, cover, and set aside for 20 minutes, or according to the package directions, to swell.

2 Meanwhile, heat the oil in a skillet and cook the onion and chicken slices over high heat for 5 minutes, turning occasionally. Reduce the heat, add the scallions, and cook for another 3-4 minutes, until softened and cooked through. Remove from the heat and keep warm.

3 In a separate skillet, heat the curry paste over low heat until softened, adding the water to loosen. Drain the couscous (if needed) and transfer to the pan with the curry paste. Toss and stir for about 2 minutes, until coated and warmed.

4 Combine the cooked chicken and onion with the curried couscous. Add the mango and cilantro, if using, and toss again before serving with spoonfuls of plain yogurt, if desired.

¾ cup barley couscous or pearl couscous (regular wheat couscous is also fine to use)
3 tablespoons olive oil
1 red onion, sliced
12 oz boneless, skinless chicken breasts, thinly sliced
bunch of scallions, cut into strips
¼ cup korma curry paste
2 tablespoons water
1 ripe mango, peeled, pitted, and cut into chunks
¼ cup chopped fresh cilantro (optional)
salt
plain yogurt, to serve (optional)

Serves **4**
Prep time **15 minutes, plus soaking**
Cooking time **15 minutes**

Minted Rice with Tomato & BEAN SPROUTS

Vegan

THE BEAN SPROUTSS IN THIS LIGHT AND FRESH STIR-FRIED RICE DISH GIVE IT A CRUNCHY BITE, WHILE THE GENEROUS ADDITION OF GARLIC ADDS A RICH, AROMATIC FLAVOR.

1 Heat the oil in a large, nonstick wok or skillet until hot, then add the scallions and garlic and stir-fry for 2–3 minutes.

2 Add the cooked rice and continue to stir-fry over high heat for 3–4 minutes. Stir in the tomatoes and mixed bean sprouts and stir-fry for another 2–3 minutes or until warmed through.

3 Remove from the heat, season to taste with salt and black pepper, then stir in the chopped mint. Serve immediately.

2 tablespoons light olive oil
6 scallions, very thinly sliced
2 garlic cloves, finely chopped
5 cups cooked, cooled basmati or other long-grain rice
2 plum tomatoes, finely chopped
2½ cups mixed bean sprouts, such as adzuki, mung, lentil, and chickpea sprouts
small handful of mint leaves, chopped
salt and black pepper

Serves **4**
Prep time **10 minutes**
Cooking time **8-10 minutes**

HEALTHY TIP

Bean sprouts are a living food, packed with valuable vitamins, minerals, and health-giving phytochemicals. They are available in some large supermarkets and health food stores. Or sprout your own—make sure you rinse them daily to keep them safe to consume.

AFFORDABILITY 1

Spicy Lentils & Chickpeas

1 Heat the oil in a heavy saucepan over medium heat, add the onion, garlic, celery, and green bell pepper, and sauté gently, stirring occasionally, for 10-12 minutes or until softened and beginning to brown.

2 Stir in the lentils and spices and cook for 2-3 minutes, stirring frequently. Add the tomato paste, broth, and chickpeas and bring to a boil. Reduce the heat, cover, and simmer gently for about 20 minutes, until the lentils collapse. Season to taste with salt and black pepper.

3 Ladle into bowls and garnish with the chopped cilantro. Serve immediately with boiled rice and spiced yogurt (see Tip below), if desired.

ACCOMPANIMENT TIP
For cooling, spiced yogurt to serve as an accompaniment, mix together 1 cup fat-free plain yogurt, 2 tablespoons lemon juice, and ½ teaspoon garam masala in a small bowl. Fold in ½ small, seeded, and grated cucumber, then season to taste with salt and black pepper. Serve sprinkled with 1 tablespoon chopped fresh cilantro.

1 tablespoon peanut oil
1 onion, finely chopped
2 garlic cloves, thinly sliced
2 celery sticks, diced
1 green bell pepper, cored, seeded, and chopped
¾ cup split red lentils, rinsed
2 teaspoons garam masala
1 teaspoon cumin seeds
½ teaspoon hot chili powder
1 teaspoon ground coriander
2 tablespoons tomato paste
3 cups Vegetable Broth (see page 244)
1 (15 oz) can chickpeas, rinsed and drained
salt and black pepper
2 tablespoons chopped fresh cilantro, to garnish

To serve (optional)
Boiled rice (see page 247)
spiced yogurt (see Tip)

Serves **4**
Prep time **15 minutes**
Cooking time **35 minutes**

LENTIL STEW
WITH GARLIC & HERB BREAD

1 Heat the oil in a large, heavy saucepan and cook the bell peppers, onion, garlic, and fennel over medium-high heat, stirring frequently, for 5 minutes, until softened and lightly browned. Stir in the lentils, broth, and wine and bring to a boil, then reduce the heat and simmer, stirring occasionally, for 25 minutes, until the lentils are tender.

2 Meanwhile, for the garlic bread, beat the butter with the garlic and thyme in a bowl and season with a little salt and black pepper. Cut the bread into thick slices, almost all the way through but leaving the bottom attached. Spread the butter thickly over each slice, then wrap the bread in aluminum foil and cook in a preheated oven, at 400°F, for 15 minutes.

3 Serve the hot stew, ladled into serving bowls, with the torn hot garlic and herb bread on the side for mopping up the juices.

¼ cup olive oil
1 red bell pepper, cored, seeded, and cut into chunks
1 green bell pepper, cored, seeded, and cut into chunks
1 red onion, coarsely chopped
1 garlic clove, sliced
1 fennel bulb, trimmed and sliced
1¼ cups green lentils, rinsed
2½ cups Vegetable Broth (see page 244)
1¼ cups nonalcoholic red wine or grape juice

Garlic bread
4 tablespoons butter, softened
1 garlic clove, crushed
2 tablespoons chopped thyme
1 whole wheat French bread
salt and black pepper

Serves **4**
Prep time **15 minutes**
Cooking time **35 minutes**

AFFORDABILITY
2

FREE WAYS TO GET FIT

You don't need to splash out on an expensive monthly gym membership to stay fit and healthy. If your budget won't stretch to paying for your stretches, there are plenty of ways you can tone up in your downtime.

RUN WILD

If you have a pair of sneakers and track pants, you can start running immediately. It's easy to fit into college life, because you won't be pinned down to certain days and times. Begin with a gentle jog around the block or campus and slowly build up to longer runs.

PULL ON YOUR GARDENING GLOVES

Got a green space? If you're lucky enough to have some outside space in your college accommodations, chances are it won't be entered into any competitions at a flower show. It might be a stereotype but students don't tend to get overexcited about flowering plants. You might clear a space in the undergrowth for a disposable BBQ, but otherwise any green space will be largely unloved. But gardening is great exercise and there's the added advantage of having something to show for your efforts.

WORKOUT IN THE LIBRARY

Well not literally… but you can borrow exercise DVDs and have a workout in the privacy of your living room. Alternatively, there are literally thousands of routines for every imaginable type of keep fit available on the Internet—just don't fall into the trap of spending more time surfing than exercising.

SAY BYE TO THE BUS

Walking is a great way to get fit without breaking into a sweat. A brisk 20-minute walk in the morning will set you up for the day and give you time to get your thoughts in order. So, if you usually travel to college by bus, put your fare back in your pocket and use your legs instead. It's free, you don't need any special equipment, and it gets you from A to B — what's not to like?

HIT THE DANCE FLOOR

If you're used to sedentary social activities, it might be time to get your butt out of the the chair and start throwing some shapes. Dancing burns plenty of calories but hopefully you'll be having such a good time that you won't notice.

ADOPT A DOG

You probably won't have a dog living with you—colleges (and landlords) tend to ban students from keeping pets. However, you could offer your services as a dog walker and benefit from plenty of exercise and fresh air, as well as earning some money.

ROASTED TOMATO & FAVA
BEAN TABBOULEH

Vegan

1 Arrange the tomato halves, cut side up, in a roasting pan. Sprinkle with the oregano, sugar, and a little black pepper. Drizzle with 1 tablespoon of the oil and roast in a preheated oven, at 350°F, for 1 hour.

2 Meanwhile, put the bulgur wheat into a saucepan with the bouillon powder and cover with the water. Bring to a gentle simmer, cover with a lid, and cook for 15 minutes, until the bulgur wheat is tender and the water absorbed. Remove from the heat, drain off any excess water, then turn into a bowl. Stir in the cumin and pumpkin or sunflower seeds. Let cool.

3 Cook the fava beans in a small saucepan of boiling water for 3 minutes. Drain, then add to the bulgur wheat mixture with the parsley, the remaining oil, and the lemon juice. Stir in the roasted tomatoes along with any juices and serve.

4 tomatoes, halved
good pinch of dried oregano
½ teaspoon granulated sugar
2 tablespoons olive oil
⅔ cup bulgur wheat, rinsed
1 teaspoon vegetable bouillon powder
2½ cups water
1 teaspoon cumin seeds
3 tablespoons pumpkin or sunflower seeds
⅔ cup frozen baby fava beans
¼ cup chopped parsley
squeeze of lemon juice
black pepper

Serves **2**
Prep time **10 minutes**
Cooking time **1 hour**

BROILED HALOUMI
WITH WARM COUSCOUS SALAD Ⓥ

1 Put the couscous into a bowl and add enough boiling water to cover by ½ inch. Season lightly with salt and let the couscous absorb the water for 10 minutes, or according to the package directions.

2 Meanwhile, heat 3 tablespoons of the oil in a large skillet and cook the onions and two-thirds of the chile over medium heat, stirring, for 4-5 minutes, until softened. Add the chickpeas and tomatoes and cook over high heat, stirring occasionally, for 3 minutes, until the chickpeas are heated through and the tomatoes are softened but still retaining their shape.

3 Meanwhile, mix the remaining oil and chile with the herbs in a shallow bowl. Add the haloumi slices and toss to coat. Place the haloumi slices on a broiler rack lined with aluminum foil and cook under a preheated hot broiler for 2-3 minutes, until browned in places.

4 Stir the couscous into the chickpea mixture and cook for 1 minute to heat through. Serve the couscous piled onto serving plates, topped with the broiled haloumi slices.

1 cup couscous
⅓ cup olive oil
2 red onions, thinly sliced
1 red chile, coarsely chopped
1 (15 oz) can chickpeas, rinsed and drained
10 cherry tomatoes, halved
3 tablespoons chopped parsley
1 tablespoon finely chopped thyme leaves
12 oz haloumi, Muenster, or mozzarella cheese, thickly sliced
salt

Serves **4**
Prep time **15 minutes, plus soaking**
Cooking time **10 minutes**

Lentil Moussaka (V)

1. Put the lentils into a saucepan with the tomatoes, garlic, oregano, and nutmeg. Pour in the broth. Bring to a boil, then reduce the heat and simmer for 20 minutes, until the lentils are tender but not mushy, topping off with extra broth as needed.

2. Meanwhile, heat the oil in a skillet and lightly sauté the eggplant slices and onion until the onion is soft and the eggplant is golden on both sides.

3. Layer the eggplant mixture and lentil mixture alternately in an ovenproof dish.

4. Make the topping. In a bowl, beat together the egg, cream cheese, and nutmeg with a good dash of salt and black pepper. Pour it over the moussaka and cook in a preheated oven, at 400°F, for 20–25 minutes or until golden and bubbling. Remove from the oven and let stand for 5 minutes before serving with a mixed leaf salad.

VARIATION

For moussaka baked potatoes, bake 4 scrubbed large baking potatoes, such as russets, in a preheated oven, at 400°F, for about 1 hour, until cooked and tender (or microwave them, if preferred). Meanwhile, make the lentil mixture as above. Sauté the eggplant slices and onion separately, then stir into the lentils when cooked. Spoon over the halved potatoes, then top each one with a spoonful of cream cheese and a sprinkling of grated cheddar-style cheese.

⅔ cup brown or green lentils, rinsed
1 (14½ oz) can diced tomatoes
2 garlic cloves, crushed
½ teaspoon dried oregano
pinch of ground (or freshly grated) nutmeg
⅔ cup Vegetable Broth (see page 244)
2–3 tablespoons vegetable oil
1 small eggplant, sliced
1 onion, finely chopped
mixed leaf salad, to serve

Cheese topping
1 egg
⅔ cup cream cheese
pinch of ground (or freshly grated) nutmeg
salt and black pepper

Serves **4**
Prep time **10 minutes**
Cooking time **45 minutes, plus standing**

LAYERED LENTIL & QUINOA
NUT ROAST (V)

1. Cook the quinoa in a saucepan of boiling water for 15-20 minutes, or according to the package directions, until tender. Drain thoroughly and transfer to a bowl.

2. Heat the oil in a separate saucepan and sauté the onion for 5 minutes to soften. Transfer half of the mixture to the bowl of quinoa. Add the celery to the pan and cook for 2 minutes. Stir in the spice, lentils, and broth and bring to a boil. Reduce the heat to a gentle simmer and cook, uncovered, for 10 minutes or until the mixture is dry and the lentils are tender. Remove from the heat, stir in the dates, and let cool.

3. Crumble the almonds into the quinoa. Beat in the cilantro, whole egg, and a little salt and black pepper. Beat the egg yolk into the cooled lentil mixture.

4. Oil an 8½ x 4½ inch loaf pan and line the bottom and long sides with strips of nonstick parchment paper.

5. Spoon half of the quinoa mixture into the prepared pan and press down firmly. Spoon half of the lentil mixture on top and level the surface. Add the remaining quinoa and lentil mixtures, spreading them evenly.

6. Bake in a preheated oven, at 350°F, for 30 minutes, until the loaf feels firm. Turn out onto a board and serve in slices.

½ cup quinoa, rinsed
1 tablespoon olive oil, plus extra
 for greasing
1 onion, finely chopped
1 celery stick, chopped
2 teaspoons ras el hanout spice
½ cups split red lentils, rinsed
1¼ cups Vegetable Broth
 (see page 244)
3 tablespoons finely chopped
 pitted dried dates
½ cup slivered almonds
2 tablespoons finely chopped
 fresh cilantro
1 egg, beaten
1 egg yolk
salt and black pepper

Serves **8**
Prep time **25 minutes,
plus cooling**
Cooking time **1 hour 10 minutes**

AFFORDABILITY
1

HOME-BAKED BEANS *Vegan*

THESE HOME-BAKED BEANS ARE EVEN BETTER MADE A DAY AHEAD,
THEN KEPT REFRIGERATED OVERNIGHT AND HEATED THROUGH UNTIL
PIPING HOT BEFORE SERVING.

1 Put all the ingredients into a Dutch oven or flameproof
casserole with a little salt and black pepper. Cover and
bring slowly to a boil.

2 Transfer to a preheated oven, at 325°F, and bake for
1½ hours. Remove the lid, stir, then bake for another
30 minutes, until the sauce is syrupy. Serve with hot
buttered toast, if desired.

VARIATION

For home-baked beans with baked potatoes, scrub 4 baking
potatoes, such as russets, then bake in a preheated oven, at
400°F, for about 1 hour, until cooked and tender (or microwave
them, if preferred). Cut the potatoes in half lengthwise, season
with salt and black pepper, and then spoon the home-baked
beans over them. Grate a little cheddar-style cheese on top
before serving.

2 (15 oz) cans cranberry or pinto
   beans, rinsed and drained
1 garlic clove, crushed
1 onion, finely chopped
2 cups Vegetable Broth
   (see page 244)
1¼ cups tomato puree or
   tomato sauce
2 tablespoons molasses
2 tablespoons tomato paste
2 tablespoons packed
   dark brown sugar
1 tablespoon Dijon mustard
1 tablespoon red wine vinegar
salt and black pepper
hot buttered toast, to serve
   (optional)

Serves **4**
Prep time **10 minutes**
Cooking time **2 hours 10 minutes**

AFFORDABILITY
1

ROASTED ROOTS
and quinoa salad (Vegan)

1. Put the beet and carrots into a roasting pan. Drizzle with the olive oil, sprinkle with the cumin seeds, and season well with salt and black pepper, then toss until the vegetables are evenly coated in the oil. Roast in a preheated oven, at 400°F, for 30-35 minutes, until tender.

2. Meanwhile, cook the quinoa in a saucepan of boiling water for 10-12 minutes, or according to the package directions, until tender, then drain. Transfer to a large bowl, add the chickpeas, onion, mint, and hazelnuts, and toss together.

3. Mix the lime juice, tamari or soy sauce, and sesame oil together in a small bowl, pour the dressing over the quinoa mixture, and gently toss together. Add the roasted beets and carrots and lightly mix through, then serve.

VARIATION

For roasted carrot and parsnip salad with edamame (soybeans), toss 10 oz each of scrubbed baby carrots and baby parsnips with 1 tablespoon olive oil, 1 teaspoon cumin seeds, and salt and black pepper in a roasting pan. Roast in a preheated oven, at 400°F, for 20-25 minutes, until tender. Meanwhile, cook the quinoa as above, adding 1 cup frozen edamame (soybeans) for the final 3 minutes of the cooking time. Drain and transfer to a large bowl. Add 1 thinly sliced red onion, a handful of coarsely chopped flat leaf parsley, and 2 tablespoons toasted blanched almonds, coarsely chopped. Make the lime juice dressing as above, pour it over the quinoa mixture, and gently toss together. Add the roasted carrots and parsnips and lightly mix through.

10 oz raw baby beets, scrubbed and halved or quartered if large
10 oz baby carrots, scrubbed
1 tablespoon olive oil
1 teaspoon cumin seeds
1 cup quinoa, rinsed
1 (15 oz) can chickpeas, rinsed and drained
1 small red onion, thinly sliced
small handful of mint leaves, coarsely chopped
2 tablespoons blanched hazelnuts, coarsely chopped
juice of 1 lime
1 tablespoon tamari or soy sauce
1 teaspoon sesame oil
salt and black pepper

Serves **4**
Prep time **10 minutes**
Cooking time **30-35 minutes**

AFFORDABILITY 1

Super Salads, Snacks & Sides

SALMON & RICE BALLS

FATTOUSH SALAD

CRAB & GRAPEFRUIT SALAD

SPICY KALE

COCONUT NOODLES IN A MUG

1 Mix together the scallions, zucchini, and oil in a large, microwave-proof mug and microwave on medium power for 2 minutes.

2 Stir in the coconut milk, bouillon powder, Thai spice, turmeric, if using, and the boiling water. Microwave on medium power for 1 minute.

3 Break the noodles into the mug and stir to mix. Microwave on medium power for 1 minute. Stir again and microwave on medium power for another 1½ minutes, until the noodles are tender. Sprinkle with the cashew nuts and serve.

3 scallions, thinly sliced
1 small zucchini, shredded
1 teaspoon wok oil or sunflower oil
½ cup coconut milk
¼ teaspoon vegetable bouillon powder
½ teaspoon Thai spice powder, such as Thai seve spice or Thai fivespice
good pinch of ground turmeric (optional)
⅓ cup boiling water
1 oz vermicelli rice noodles
10 cashew nuts, coarsely chopped

Makes **1**
Prep time **5 minutes**
Cooking time **5½ minutes**

MASSAMAN LENTILS
with Cauliflower ⓥ

1 Cook the lentils in a saucepan of boiling water for 15 minutes, until softened but not falling apart. Drain well.

2 Meanwhile, melt the butter with the oil in a separate saucepan. Add the onions and carrot and sauté gently for 5 minutes, stirring frequently. Add the cauliflower and cook for another 5 minutes.

3 Stir in the curry paste, sugar, ginger, and broth and bring to a gentle simmer. Cook gently, stirring frequently, for 10 minutes, until the cauliflower is tender.

4 Stir in the lentils and basil, season to taste with salt and black pepper, and then serve with boiled jasmine or long-grain rice.

¾ cup green lentils, rinsed
1½ tablespoons butter
1 teaspoon vegetable oil
2 onions, sliced
1 large carrot, thinly sliced
1 small cauliflower or ½ large cauliflower, cut into large florets
1 tablespoon Massaman curry paste
1 teaspoon packed light brown or granulated sugar
¾ inch piece of fresh ginger root, peeled and grated
2 cups Vegetable Broth (see page 244)
small handful of Thai basil, torn into pieces
salt and black pepper
Boiled Rice (see page 247), to serve

Serves **2**
Prep time **10 minutes**
Cooking time **20 minutes**

QUICK CURRIED EGG SALAD Ⓥ

1 Shell, then halve the eggs and place on a large plate with the tomatoes, lettuce leaves, and cucumber.

2 Mix the yogurt with the curry powder, tomato paste, lime juice, and mayonnaise in a small bowl. Season the dressing with salt and black pepper to taste, then pour it over the salad. Serve immediately, garnished with thyme leaves.

8 hard-boiled eggs
4 tomatoes, cut into wedges
2 Bibb, Boston, or other small butterhead lettuce, leaves separated
½ cucumber, sliced
1 cup plain yogurt
1 tablespoon mild curry powder
3 tablespoons tomato paste
juice of 2 limes
⅓ cup mayonnaise
salt and black pepper
thyme leaves, to garnish

Serves **4**
Prep time **10 minutes**

AFFORDABILITY 1

HEALTHY TIP

SNACK ATTACK Keep a cereal bar, piece of fresh fruit, some dried fruit, or a snack bag of unsalted nuts or seeds in your bag for when you have a sudden energy slump. If there's a healthy snack on hand, you'll be less tempted to raid the cafeteria for a doughnut (see page 74 for healthy snack ideas).

ROASTED VEGETABLE COUSCOUS SALAD

1 Place all the vegetables in a large nonstick baking pan in a single layer. Drizzle with a little oil and season well with salt and black pepper. Roast in a preheated oven, at 400°F, for 15-20 minutes or until the edges of the vegetables are just starting to char.

2 Meanwhile, put the couscous into a wide bowl and pour over enough boiling water to just cover. Season well. Cover with plastic wrap and let stand, undisturbed, for 10 minutes, or according to the package directions, until all the liquid has been absorbed. Fluff up the grains with a fork and place on a wide, shallow serving platter.

3 Make the dressing by mixing together the orange juice, oil, cumin and cinnamon and season well with salt and black pepper.

4 Fold the roasted vegetables, preserved lemons, and herbs into the couscous, pour the dressing over the top, and toss to mix well.

5 Sprinkle with the pine nuts, feta, and pomegranate seeds and serve immediately.

1 red bell pepper, seeded and cut into 1 inch pieces
1 yellow bell pepper, seeded and cut into 1 inch pieces
1 eggplant, cut into 1 inch pieces
1 zucchini, cut into 1 inch cubes
2 small red onions, cut into thick wedges
olive oil, to drizzle
1 cup couscous
6-8 preserved lemons, halved
large handful of mint and cilantro leaves, chopped
1/3 cup pine nuts, toasted
1 cup crumbled feta cheese
1/2 cup pomegranate seeds
salt and black pepper

Dressing
juice of 1 orange
1/3 cup olive oil
1 teaspoon ground cumin
1 teaspoon ground cinnamon

Serves **4**
Prep time **15 minutes**
Cooking time **15-20 minutes**

FATTOUSH SALAD

1 First make the dressing. Whisk the oil, lemon juice, garlic, and sumac or cumin together in a bowl. Season to taste with salt and black pepper.

2 To make the salad, combine the pita pieces, tomatoes, cucumber, radishes, onion, lettuce leaves, and mint leaves in a large bowl.

3 Pour the dressing over the salad and gently mix together to coat the salad evenly.

1 pita bread, torn into small pieces
6 plum tomatoes, seeded and coarsely chopped
1 cucumber, peeled and coarsely chopped
10 radishes, sliced
1 red onion, coarsely chopped
1 Bibb, Boston, or other small butterhead lettuce, leaves torn
small handful of fresh mint leaves

Dressing
1 cup olive oil
juice of 3 lemons
1 garlic clove, crushed
2 teaspoons sumac or 2 teaspoons ground cumin
salt and black pepper

Serves **4**
Prep time **15 minutes**

Tricolore Avocado & Couscous Salad

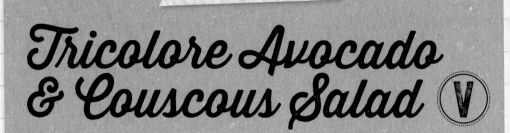

1. Mix the couscous and broth or boiling water together in a bowl, then cover with plastic wrap and let stand for 10 minutes, or according to the package directions.

2. Meanwhile, to make the dressing, mix the pesto with the lemon juice in a small bowl. Season with salt and black pepper, then gradually mix in the oil.

3. Pour the dressing over the couscous and mix with a fork. Add the tomatoes, avocados, and mozzarella to the couscous, mix well, then lightly stir in the arugula. Serve.

1 cup couscous
1¼ cups hot Vegetable Broth (see page 244) or boiling water
16 cherry tomatoes
2 ripe avocados, peeled, pitted, and chopped
1½ cups drained and chopped mozzarella cheese
handful of arugula

Dressing
2 tablespoons Pesto (see page 248)
1 tablespoon lemon juice
¼ cup extra virgin olive oil
salt and black pepper

Serves **4**
Prep time **20 minutes**

Italian
BROCCOLI & EGG SALAD

1 Put the broccoli in the top of a steamer, cook for 3 minutes, then add the leeks and cook for another 2 minutes.

2 Mix together the lemon juice, oil, honey, capers, and chopped tarragon in a salad bowl and season to taste with salt and black pepper. Shell and coarsely chop the eggs.

3 Add the broccoli and leeks to the dressing, toss together, and then sprinkle with the chopped eggs. Garnish with tarragon sprigs and serve warm with extra-thick slices of whole wheat bread, if desired.

VARIATION
For a broccoli, cauliflower, and egg salad, use ¼ head of broccoli and ¼ head of cauliflower instead of ½ head of broccoli. Cut the cauliflower into small florets and steam with the broccoli. Serve with a blue cheese dressing made by mixing together ½ cup crumbled blue cheese, 6 chopped sun-dried tomatoes, and 3 tablespoons balsamic vinegar.

½ head of broccoli, cut into florets and stems thickly sliced
2 leeks, trimmed, cleaned, and thickly sliced
¼ cup lemon juice
2 tablespoons olive oil
2 teaspoons honey
1 tablespoon capers, drained
2 tablespoons chopped tarragon, plus extra sprigs to garnish
4 hard-boiled eggs
salt and black pepper
extra-thick slices of whole wheat bread, to serve (optional)

Serves **4**
Prep time **15 minutes**
Cooking time **5 minutes**

GREEK SALAD
WITH TOASTED PITA (V)

1 Put the feta, mint, olives, tomatoes, lemon juice, onion, and oregano into a bowl and toss together to mix.

2 Toast the pita breads under a preheated hot broiler, turning once, until lightly golden, then cut open and toast the open sides. Or cut open and toast in a toaster until lightly golden.

3 Tear the hot pitas into bite-size pieces, then toss with the other ingredients in the bowl. Serve immediately with lemon wedges.

^{2}/$_3$ cup crumbled feta cheese
   (crumbled into smallish chunks)
8-10 fresh mint leaves, shredded
1 cup pitted kalamata olives
2 tomatoes, chopped
juice of 1 large lemon
1 small red onion, thinly sliced
1 teaspoon dried oregano
4 pita breads
lemon wedges, to serve

Serves **4**
Prep time **15 minutes**
Cooking time **5 minutes**

HEALTHY TIP
SWITCH REGULAR SOFT DRINKS FOR LOW-CALORIE VERSIONS
Carbonated drinks aren't exactly a healthy addition to your diet, but if you're going to treat yourself, at least make it sugar-free.

SMOKED MACKEREL SUPERFOOD SALAD

1 Put the squash into a roasting pan and sprinkle with 1 tablespoon of the oil and the cumin seeds. Put into a preheated oven, at 400°F, for 15-18 minutes, until tender. Let cool slightly.

2 Meanwhile, cook the broccoli in a saucepan of boiling water for 4-5 minutes, until tender, adding the peas 3 minutes before the end of the cooking time. Remove with a slotted spoon and refresh under cold running water, then drain (reserving the cooking water). Cook the quinoa in the broccoli water for 15 minutes, or according to the package directions, then drain and let cool slightly.

3 Heat a nonstick skillet over medium-low heat and dry-fry the seeds, stirring frequently, until golden brown and toasted. Set aside. Heat the mackerel fillets according to the package directions, then skin and break into flakes.

4 Whisk together the remaining oil, the lemon juice, honey, and mustard in a small bowl. Toss together all the ingredients, except the sprouts, with the dressing in a serving bowl. Serve topped with the sprouts.

½ butternut squash, peeled, seeded, and cut into ½ inch cubes
¼ cup olive oil
1 teaspoon cumin seeds
1 head of broccoli, cut into florets
1½ cups frozen or fresh peas
3 tablespoons quinoa, rinsed
¼ cup mixed seeds
2 smoked mackerel fillets
juice of 1 lemon
1 teaspoon honey
1 Dijon mustard
1 cup shredded red cabbage
4 tomatoes, chopped
4 cooked beets, cut into wedges
⅔ cup radish or alfalfa sprouts

Serves **4**
Prep time **20 minutes**
Cooking time **25-30 minutes**

AFFORDABILITY 2

ZUCCHINI, FETA & MINT SALAD

V

AFFORDABILITY **1**

1. Thinly slice the zucchini lengthwise into long ribbons. Drizzle with oil and season with salt and black pepper. Heat a ridged grill pan until hot, then grill the zucchini, in batches, until tender and with grill marks on both sides. Transfer to a large salad bowl.

2. Make the dressing by whisking together the oil and lemon zest and juice in a small bowl. Season to taste with salt and black pepper.

3. Coarsely chop the mint, reserving some leaves for the garnish. Carefully mix together the grilled zucchini, chopped mint, and dressing in the salad bowl, then sprinkle the feta over the top, garnish with the remaining mint leaves, and serve.

VARIATION

For marinated zucchini salad, thinly slice 3 zucchini lengthwise and put them into a nonmetallic bowl with ½ seeded and sliced red chile ¼ cup lemon juice, 1 crushed garlic clove, and ¼ cup olive oil. Season to taste with salt and black pepper. Let the salad marinate, covered, for at least 1 hour. Coarsely chop a small bunch of mint leaves, toss with the salad, and serve immediately.

3 green zucchini
2 yellow zucchini
olive oil, for drizzling
small bunch of mint leaves
⅓ cup crumbled feta cheese
salt and black pepper

Dressing
2 tablespoons olive oil
finely grated zest and juice of
  1 lemon

Serves **4**
Prep time **15 minutes**
Cooking time **10 minutes**

BRAINFOOD BOWL

1 Cook the rice in a large saucepan of lightly salted water for 25 minutes or until just tender.

2 Meanwhile, cut the broccoli into smaller pieces and cook in a separate saucepan of boiling water for 2 minutes, until softened. Add the sugar snap peas and cook for another 30 seconds. Drain, rinse under cold running water, then drain again.

3 Lightly toast the hazelnuts in a dry skillet, shaking the pan frequently until the nuts start to brown. Add the pumpkin seeds and cook for another 1-2 minutes, until they start to pop.

4 Thoroughly drain the rice and mix in a bowl with the broccoli, sugar snap peas, nuts, and seeds.

5 Halve the grapefruit. Squeeze the juice from one half into a small bowl. Cut away the skin and white pith from the remaining half and chop the flesh. Add to the rice bowl. Halve, pit, peel, and dice the avocado and add to the grapefruit juice. Toss to coat, then lift out with a slotted spoon and add to the rice.

6 Whisk the ginger, oil, and honey into the grapefruit juice. Stir the dressing into the rice mixture just before serving. Season to taste with salt and black pepper and serve.

½ cup brown rice
2 cups broccoli florets
1 cup diagonally halved sugar snap peas
½ cup coarsely chopped hazelnuts
3 tablespoons pumpkin seeds
1 pink or red grapefruit
1 ripe avocado
½ cup peeled and grated fresh ginger root
1 tablespoon olive oil
1 tablespoon honey
salt and black pepper

Serves **2**
Prep time **20 minutes**
Cooking time **25 minutes**

SOY TOFU SALAD
WITH CILANTRO

1 Cut the tofu into bite-size cubes and carefully arrange on a serving plate in a single layer. Sprinkle with the scallions, cilantro, and chile.

2 Drizzle with the soy sauce and oil, then let stand at room temperature for 10 minutes before serving.

VARIATION

For steamed chile-soy tofu, drain 1 lb firm tofu, cut it into bite-size cubes, and put onto a heatproof plate that will fit inside a bamboo steamer. Cover and steam over a wok or large saucepan of boiling water for 20 minutes, then drain off the excess water and carefully transfer to a serving plate. Heat ¼ cup light soy sauce, 1 tablespoon each sesame oil and peanut oil, and 2 teaspoons oyster sauce in a small saucepan until hot. Pour the sauce over the tofu, sprinkle with 4 thinly sliced scallions, 1 finely chopped red chile, and a small handful of finely chopped fresh cilantro leaves, and serve.

1 lb firm tofu, drained
6 scallions, finely shredded
large handful of fresh cilantro leaves, coarsely chopped
1 large mild red chile, seeded and thinly sliced
¼ cup light soy sauce
2 teaspoons sesame oil

Serves **4**
Prep time **10 minutes, plus standing**

SPICED CHICKEN & MANGO SALAD

1 Put 4 teaspoons of the curry paste into a plastic food bag with the lemon juice and mix together by squeezing the bag. Add the chicken pieces and toss together.

2 Fill the bottom of a steamer halfway with water and bring to a boil. Remove the chicken from the bag and place in the top of the steamer in a single layer. Cover and steam for 5-6 minutes, until cooked through.

3 Meanwhile, mix the remaining curry paste in a bowl with the yogurt. Put the mango, watercress, cucumber, and onion into a bowl, add the yogurt dressing, and toss together gently.

4 Tear the lettuce into pieces, divide it among 4 plates, then spoon the mango mixture on top. Add the warm chicken strips on top, then serve.

VARIATION
For spiced chicken sandwich filling, mix the curry paste and yogurt with ¼ cup reduced-fat mayonnaise. Stir in 3½ cups cold diced cooked chicken and ¼ cup golden raisins. Sprinkle with ¼ cup toasted slivered almonds and serve on a bed of mixed salad and herb greens.

⅓ cup mild curry paste
juice of 1 lemon
4 small boneless, skinless chicken breasts, cut into long, thin strips
⅔ cup plain yogurt
1 ripe mango, peeled, pitted, and cut into bite-size chunks
½ bunch watercress or 2 cups peppery green, torn into smaller pieces
½ cucumber, diced
½ red onion, chopped
½ iceberg lettuce

Serves **4**
Prep time **5 minutes**
Cooking time **5-6 minutes**

AFFORDABILITY
3

TANDOORI CHICKEN

1   Mix the yogurt, lemon juice, spices, tomato paste, garlic, and ginger together in a shallow, nonmetallic dish. Add the chicken and toss to coat. Cover and let marinate in the refrigerator for 3-4 hours or until required.

2   When you are ready to serve, heat the oil in a large skillet. Lift the chicken out of the marinade and add to the pan. Cook over medium heat for 8-10 minutes, turning occasionally, until the chicken is browned and cooked through.

3   Meanwhile, for the salad, toss the salad greens, cilantro, and lemon juice together in a bowl and then divide among serving plates. Spoon the hot chicken on top and serve immediately.

VARIATION

For tandoori chicken skewers, thread 12 oz diced boneless, skinless chicken breasts onto 8 wooden skewers soaked in water for 30 minutes. Place in a large, shallow, nonmetallic dish, then spoon the yogurt marinade over the poultry and chill as above. When you are ready to serve, lift the kebabs out of the marinade and cook under a preheated hot broiler, turning occasionally, until the chicken is cooked through. Serve with the salad dressed with lemon juice as above.

1 cup plain yogurt
2 tablespoons lemon juice
½ teaspoon ground turmeric
1 teaspoon garam masala
1 teaspoon cumin seeds, coarsely
   crushed
2 tablespoons tomato paste
2 garlic cloves, finely chopped
¾ inch piece of fresh ginger root,
   peeled and finely chopped
3 boneless, skinless chicken
   breasts, thickly sliced
1 tablespoon sunflower oil

Salad
1 (7 oz) package mixed
   salad greens
small bunch of fresh cilantro
¼ cup lemon juice

Serves **4**
Prep time **15 minutes,
plus marinating**
Cooking time **10 minutes**

TURKEY & AVOCADO SALAD

1 large ripe avocado, peeled,
  pitted, and diced
large handful of microgreens or
  alfalfa sprouts
5 cups mixed salad greens
2²/₃ cups thinly sliced
  cooked turkey
¹/₃ cup mixed toasted seeds, such
  as pumpkin and sunflower
toasted rye bread or flatbreads,
  to serve

Dressing
2 tablespoons apple juice
2 tablespoons plain yogurt
1 teaspoon honey
1 teaspoon whole-grain mustard
salt and black pepper

Serves **4**
Prep time **15 minutes**

1 Put the avocado, microgreens, and salad greens
  in a large bowl and mix together. Add the turkey and
  toasted seeds and stir to combine.

2 Make the dressing by whisking together the apple juice,
  yogurt, honey, and mustard in a small bowl. Season to
  taste with salt and black pepper.

3 Pour the dressing over the salad and toss to mix.
  Serve the salad with toasted rye bread or rolled up
  in flatbreads.

VARIATION
For a crab, apple, and avocado salad, prepare the salad in the
same way, using 2 cups cooked, fresh white crabmeat instead
of the turkey. Cut 1 peeled and cored, sweet crisp apple into
thin matchsticks and toss with a little lemon juice to stop it
from discoloring. Add to the crab salad. Make a dressing by
whisking together 2 tablespoons apple juice, 3 tablespoons
olive oil, a squeeze of lemon juice, and 1 finely diced shallot.
Season to taste with salt and black pepper. Pour the dressing
over the salad, stir carefully to mix, and serve.

TUNA & CRANBERRY BEAN SALAD

1 Heat the cranberry beans in a saucepan over medium heat for 3 minutes, adding the water if the beans start to stick to the bottom of the pan.

2 Put the oil, garlic, and chile into a large bowl. Stir in the celery, onion, and hot beans and season with salt and black pepper. Cover and let marinate at room temperature for at least 30 minutes and up to 4 hours.

3 Stir in the tuna and lemon zest and juice. Gently toss in the arugula, taste, and adjust the seasoning with extra salt, pepper, and lemon juice, if necessary, then serve.

VARIATION
For a mixed bean salad, heat the cranberry beans, as above, with 1 (15 oz) can rinsed and drained white kidney (cannellini) beans. Let marinate with the other salad ingredients as above, but also adding 2 tablespoons coarsely chopped flat leaf parsley. After marinating, toss in 2 cups mâche or peppery greens, season with salt and black pepper, and serve.

1 (15 oz) can cranberry or pinto
  beans, rinsed and drained
1 tablespoon water (optional)
2 tablespoons extra virgin olive oil
2 garlic cloves, crushed
1 red chile, seeded and finely
  chopped
2 celery sticks, thinly sliced
½ red onion, cut into thin wedges
1 (5 oz) can tuna in olive oil,
  drained and flaked
finely grated zest and juice of
  1 lemon
2 cups arugula leaves
salt and black pepper

Serves **4**
Prep time **15 minutes,
plus marinating**
Cooking time **3 minutes**

Crab & Grapefruit

SALAD

1 Combine the crabmeat, grapefruit, arugula, scallions, and snow peas in a serving dish. Season to taste with salt and black pepper.

2 Make the dressing by whisking together the watercress, mustard, and oil in a small bowl. Season to taste with salt.

3 Toast the chapattis. Stir the dressing into the crab salad, then serve with the toasted chapattis and lime wedges on the side.

VARIATION
For a shrimp, potato, and asparagus salad, substitute 12 oz cooked peeled shrimp for the crab and 4 oz asparagus, cooked, for the grapefruit, and add 8 oz cooked and cooled new potatoes.

12 oz cooked white crabmeat
1 pink grapefruit, peeled, white pith removed and flesh sliced
2 cups arugula
3 scallions, sliced
3 cups halved snow peas
salt and black pepper

Watercress dressing
1 bunch of watercress, tough stems removed, chopped
1 tablespoon Dijon mustard
2 tablespoons olive oil

To serve
4 chapattis
lime wedges

Serves **4**
Prep time **15 minutes**

QUICK ONE-PAN
RATATOUILLE

Vegan

1 Heat the oil in a large saucepan until hot. Add the onions, eggplant, zucchini, bell peppers, and garlic and cook, stirring constantly, for a few minutes, until softened.

2 Add the tomatoes, season with salt and black pepper, and stir well. Reduce the heat, cover the pan tightly, and simmer for 15 minutes, until all the vegetables are cooked. Remove from the heat and stir in the parsley or basil before serving.

½ cup olive oil
2 onions, chopped
1 eggplant, cut into bite-size cubes
2 large zucchini, cut into
  bite-size pieces
1 red bell pepper, cored, seeded,
  and cut into bite-size pieces
1 yellow bell pepper, cored, seeded,
  and cut into bite-size pieces
2 garlic cloves, crushed
1 (14½ oz) can diced tomatoes
¼ cup chopped parsley or basil
salt and black pepper

Serves **4**
Prep time **10 minutes**
Cooking time **20 minutes**

AFFORDABILITY
1

GOAT CHEESE & SPINACH
QUESADILLAS (V)

1 Put the spinach in a saucepan with a small amount of water, then cover and cook until wilted. Drain and squeeze dry.

2 Heat a nonstick skillet over medium heat until hot, add 1 tortilla, and then crumble one-quarter of the goat cheese, followed by one-quarter of the spinach and sun-dried tomatoes, over the tortilla. Season lightly with salt and black pepper.

3 Place 1 tortilla on top and cook for 3-4 minutes, until golden underneath. Carefully turn the quesadilla over and cook for another 3-4 minutes. Remove from the pan and keep warm. Repeat with the remaining 6 tortillas.

4 Meanwhile, mix together the avocados, onion, lime juice, and cilantro in a bowl.

5 Serve the warm quesadillas cut into wedges with the avocado salsa.

9 cups baby spinach leaves or 1 (10 oz) package spinach, thawed if frozen
8 soft flour tortillas
8 oz goat cheese
2 tablespoons drained, chopped sun-dried tomatoes
2 ripe avocados, peeled, pitted, and diced
1 red onion, thinly sliced
juice of 1 lime
2 tablespoons chopped fresh cilantro
salt and black pepper

Serves **4**
Prep time **10 minutes**
Cooking time **25-35 minutes**

AFFORDABILITY
2

SMOKED MACKEREL & CHIVE PÂTÉ

1 Put the mackerel and cream cheese into a bowl and mash together well. Add all the remaining ingredients and mix well. Alternatively, mix all the ingredients together in a blender or food processor.

2 Spoon the mixture into 8 small individual serving dishes or 1 large serving dish. Cover and refrigerate for at least 2 hours or up to 4 hours, before serving.

3 Serve the mackerel pâté with vegetable sticks and whole wheat toast, if desired.

VARIATION
Try using other omega-3-rich fish instead of mackerel in this recipe, such as canned (in water) drained sardines, salmon, or tuna.

7 oz smoked mackerel, skinned, boned and flaked
½ cup low-fat cream cheese
bunch of chives, snipped
1 tablespoon fat-free vinaigrette
1 tablespoon lemon juice
vegetable sticks and whole wheat toast, to serve (optional)

Serves **8**
Prep time **10 minutes, plus chilling**

HEALTHY TIP

Of all the oily fish that are readily available, mackerel is the richest source of omega-3 fatty acids, so enjoy it in all its many forms— fresh, canned, or smoked. It is also one of the least expensive oily fish.

HOT & SMOKY HUMMUS WITH WARM FLATBREAD

Vegan

LEBANESE FLATBREAD IS A ROUND, FLAT, SLIGHTLY PUFFY BREAD, WHICH GOES WELL WITH "MEZZE" DIPS. IF YOU CAN'T GET HOLD OF IT, PITAS OR EVEN SOFT FLOUR TORTILLAS ARE A GOOD SUBSTITUTE.

1 Put all the ingredients, except the olive oil and sesame seeds, into a blender or food processor and process until smooth. With the machine still running, slowly drizzle the oil into the chickpea paste until it is all completely incorporated. Season to taste with salt and black pepper and then scrape the hummus into a small dish.

2 Heat a dry, nonstick skillet and toast the sesame seeds over medium-low heat, moving them quickly around the pan until they are golden brown. Stir most of the sesame seeds into the hummus, then sprinkle the rest over the top.

3 Wrap the flatbreads in aluminum foil and heat in a preheated oven, at 325°F, for about 10 minutes, until warmed through. Drizzle the hummus with olive oil, sprinkle with smoked paprika, and serve with the warm flatbreads and crunchy vegetable sticks, if desired.

1 (15 oz) can chickpeas, rinsed
  and drained
3 tablespoons lemon juice
1 large garlic clove, crushed
2 tablespoons tahini
1 teaspoon hot smoked paprika,
  plus extra for sprinkling
½ teaspoon ground cumin
⅔ cup extra virgin olive oil,
  plus extra for drizzling
2 tablespoons sesame seeds
salt and black pepper

To serve
4 Lebanese or Turkish flatbreads
crunchy raw vegetable crudités
  (optional)

Serves **4**
Prep time **15 minutes**
Cooking time **10 minutes**

AFFORDABILITY
1

FREEZER AND PANTRY MEALS

When you're short of time and money, it's time to turn to the freezer and pantry for some inspiration. You'll be amazed at the amount of food that gets pushed to the back of freezer or cupboards as new arrivals take pride of place. If you think creatively, there's generally a meal to be made from the cans, packages, and cartons that you pull out from the murky depths.

CHILI CON CARNE

- GROUND BEEF OR TURKEY
- ONION AND GARLIC (IF YOU HAVE THEM)
- CHILI POWDER
- CAN OF KIDNEY BEANS
- CAN OF DICED TOMATOES

Brown the ground meat in a large saucepan, adding chopped onion and garlic (if you have them). A dash of Worcestershire sauce, barbecue sauce, or a boullion cube will also give a flavor boost. Add the chili powder, rinsed and drained kidney beans, and the tomatoes and simmer until the meat is cooked through and the sauce reduced. Serve with Boiled Rice (see page 247).

COUSCOUS SALAD

- COUSCOUS
- CAN OF CHICKPEAS
- PAPRIKA
- SUN-DRIED TOMATOES (IF YOU HAVE THEM)

Soak the couscous according to the package directions. Add the rinsed and drained chickpeas, a dash of paprika, and some chopped sun-dried tomatoes.

CHICKPEA AND SPINACH CURRY

- SELECTION OF SPICES, SUCH AS CHILI POWDER, GARAM MASALA, MUSTARD SEEDS, GROUND TURMERIC, GROUND CORIANDER
- ONION
- CAN OF CHICKPEAS
- CAN OF CHOPPED TOMATOES
- HANDFUL OF FROZEN SPINACH

Cook the spices in a little oil, add a chopped onion, then add the rinsed and drained chickpeas and the tomatoes. Cook until the sauce thickens, then add the spinach and heat through. Serve with Boiled Rice (see page 247) or warm naan.

TARKA DHAL

- RED LENTILS OR YELLOW SPLIT PEAS, RINSED AND DRAINED
- ONION
- GARLIC
- CHILI POWDER
- CUMIN SEEDS AND GROUND TURMERIC (IF YOU HAVE THEM)

Cook the lentils according to the package directions. Meanwhile, cook a chopped onion, some garlic, and the spices in a little oil. Add the spice mix to the lentils and stir to combine.

PILAF

- ONION
- BASMATI RICE
- VEGETABLE OR CHICKEN BOUILLON CUBE
- FROZEN PEAS

Melt a little butter or oil in a large saucepan and sauté the chopped onion. Add the rice and coat in the oil, then just cover with boiling water and stir in the bouillon cube. Cover and simmer over low heat for about 10 minutes or until the rice is cooked. Stir in a handful of frozen peas just before the end of the cooking time. Fluff through the rice with a fork.

GUACAMOLE

Vegan

1 Put the avocados and lime juice in a bowl and mash together to prevent discoloration, then stir in the remaining ingredients.

2 Serve immediately with oat cakes, rice cakes, or vegetable sticks.

2 ripe avocados, peeled, pitted, and chopped
juice of 1 lime
6 cherry tomatoes, diced
1 tablespoon chopped fresh cilantro
1–2 garlic cloves, crushed
oat cakes, rice cakes, or vegetable sticks, to serve

Serves **4**
Prep time **10 minutes**

HEALTHY TIP

DOWNLOAD A PEDOMETER There are plenty of free pedometer apps available, and they are a great way to check your daily activity. Aim for 10,000 steps a day to help maintain a healthy lifestyle.

SWEET CARROT & ROSEMARY SCONES (V)

1 Grease a baking sheet and set aside.

2 Sift the flour, baking powder, and cream of tartar into a bowl or food processor, tipping in the grains left in the sifter. Stir in the rosemary and sugar. Add the butter and rub in using your fingertips or process until the mixture resembles bread crumbs. Stir in the carrots and milk and mix or process briefly to make a soft dough, adding a dash more milk if the dough feels dry.

3 Knead the dough on a lightly floured surface until smooth, then roll out to ¾ inch thick. Cut out 12 circles using a 1¼ inch plain cookie cutter or a glass, rerolling the scraps to make more. Place slightly apart on the prepared baking sheet and brush with milk.

4 Bake in a preheated oven, at 425°F, for 8-10 minutes, until risen and pale golden. Transfer to a wire rack to cool. Halve the scones and serve spread with mascarpone and fruit jelly.

VARIATION

For whole wheat apple and golden raisin scones, mix 1 cup whole wheat flour, ¾ cup white all-purpose flour, 1 teaspoon ground allspice, and 1 tablespoon baking powder in a bowl or food processor. Add 3 tablespoons slightly salted butter, chilled and diced, and rub in using your fingertips or process until the mixture resembles bread crumbs. Stir in ⅓ cup chopped golden raisins and 1 peeled, cored, and grated sweet, crisp apple or process briefly. Add ½ cup milk and mix or process briefly to make a soft dough, adding a little more milk if the dough feels dry. Roll out, shape, and bake as above.

4 tablespoons slightly salted butter, chilled and diced, plus extra for greasing
2 cups stone-ground spelt flour, plus extra for dusting
2 teaspoons baking powder
½ teaspoon cream of tartar
2 teaspoons finely chopped rosemary
2 tablespoons granulated sugar
2 carrots, grated
½ cup milk, plus extra to glaze

To serve
mascarpone cheese
fruit jelly, such as apple or grape

Makes **12**
Prep time **15 minutes,**
plus cooling
Cooking time **8-10 minutes**

AFFORDABILITY 2

SPICY ZUCCHINI FRITTERS

1 Grate the zucchini into a colander. Sprinkle lightly with salt and let stand for at least 1 hour to drain. Squeeze out the remaining liquid.

2 Put the remaining ingredients, except the eggs and oil, into a mixing bowl and add the grated zucchini. Season lightly with salt and black pepper, keeping in mind you have already salted the zucchini, and mix well. Add the eggs and mix again to combine.

3 Heat half of the oil in a large skillet over medium-high heat. Place tabelspoonfuls of the mixture (in batches), well spaced, in the pan and press down with the back of the spoon. Cook for 1-2 minutes on each side, until golden and cooked through. Remove from the pan and keep warm. Repeat to cook the rest of the fritters in the same way, adding the remaining oil to the pan when necessary. Serve warm.

ACCOMPANIMENT TIP

For a cucumber, mango, and yogurt relish, to serve as an accompaniment, peel, seed, and coarsely grate 1 cucumber into a fine mesh strainer. Squeeze out any excess liquid using the back of a spoon. Place the grated cucumber in a bowl with 2 tablespoons hot mango chutney and 1 cup fat-free Greek yogurt. Stir in a small handful of finely chopped fresh cilantro leaves, season with salt and black pepper, and chill in the refrigerator until required.

3 zucchini
2 large scallions, grated or minced
1 garlic clove, finely chopped
finely grated zest of 1 lemon
¼ cup chickpea (besan) flour
2 teaspoons medium curry powder
1 red chile, seeded and finely chopped
2 tablespoons finely chopped mint leaves
2 tablespoons finely chopped fresh cilantro leaves
2 eggs, lightly beaten
2 tablespoons light olive oil
salt and black pepper
cucumber and mango relish, to serve (see Tip)

Serves **4**
Prep time **15 minutes, plus draining**
Cooking time **10-15 minutes**

Salmon & Rice BALLS

1 Put the salmon, onion, spices, cilantro, and rice into a large bowl and mix well. Stir in the egg and season well with salt and black pepper. Mix in enough of the flour to form a stiff mixture. Using wet hands, shape into 20 small balls.

2 Heat the oil in a large skillet, add the balls, and cook for 3-4 minutes, turning once, until golden.

3 Meanwhile, mix together the yogurt, cucumber, and mint in a bowl. Serve with the hot balls.

2 (6 oz) cans salmon, drained and flaked
1 small onion, sliced
½ teaspoon ground cumin
¼ teaspoon dried red pepper flakes
2 tablespoons chopped fresh cilantro
½ cup cooked cold white rice (see page 247)
1 egg, beaten
1-2 tablespoons all-purpose flour
2 tablespoons canola oil
⅔ cup plain yogurt
½ cucumber, grated
1 tablespoon chopped mint
salt and black pepper

Serves **4**
Prep time **20 minutes**
Cooking time **5 minutes**

AFFORDABILITY 2

LIGHT **EGG-FRIED** RICE

1 Beat the eggs with the ginger and half of the soy sauce in a bowl until combined.

2 Heat the peanut oil in a nonstick wok or large skillet over high heat until the oil starts to shimmer. Pour in the egg mixture and cook, stirring constantly, for 30 seconds or until softly scrambled.

3 Add the cooked rice, scallions, sesame oil, and remaining soy sauce to the pan and toss together for 1-2 minutes, until the rice is piping hot. Serve immediately.

VARIATION
For fried rice with Chinese greens and chile, follow the recipe above, adding 1 seeded and sliced red chile and 1 cup shredded Chinese greens once the rice is piping hot, tossing together for another 30 seconds.

4 eggs
2 teaspoons peeled and finely chopped fresh ginger root
1 ½ tablespoons light soy sauce
2 tablespoons peanut oil
2 cups freshly cooked jasmine rice or long-grain rice (see page 247), cooled
2 scallions, thinly sliced
¼ teaspoon sesame oil

Serves **4**
Prep time **5 minutes**
Cooking time **5 minutes**

Spicy Kale

 *Vegan*

1 Heat the oil in a wok or large skillet over medium heat. Add the garlic and onion and sauté for 5-10 minutes or until the onion is translucent.

2 Add the curly kale and stir-fry for another 5 minutes. Stir in the lime juice and chile, season with salt and black pepper to taste, and then serve immediately.

VARIATION
For spicy cabbage, replace the curly kale with a small head of cabbage. Discard the stems and tough outer leaves, then chop the leaves before cooking with the softened garlic and onion, then finishing as above. This recipe also works well with collard greens.

1 tablespoon olive oil
1 garlic clove, crushed
1 large onion, chopped
1 lb curly kale, stems removed and leaves chopped
2 teaspoons lime juice
1 red chile, seeded and chopped
salt and black pepper

Serves **4**
Prep time **10 minutes**
Cooking time **15 minutes**

AFFORDABILITY **1**

QUICK SPINACH
WITH PINE NUTS Ⓥ

IF YOU HAVE TO WASH THE SPINACH, MAKE SURE THAT IT IS DRY BEFORE YOU START TO COOK. PLACE IT IN A SALAD SPINNER OR DISH TOWEL, AND SPIN IT AROUND TO DISPERSE ANY EXCESS WATER

1 Heat the oil in a large saucepan, add the onion and garlic, and sauté for 5 minutes.

2 Put the pine nuts into a small, heavy skillet and dry-fry until browned, stirring constantly, because they turn brown quickly. Remove from the heat.

3 Add the tomatoes, spinach, butter, and nutmeg to the onion and garlic and season with salt and black pepper. Turn up the heat to high and mix well. Cook for 3 minutes, until the spinach has just started to wilt, stirring frequently.

4 Remove from the heat, stir in the pine nuts, and serve immediately.

1 tablespoon olive oil
1 red onion, sliced
1 garlic clove, crushed
2/3 cup pine nuts
4 tomatoes, skinned, cored, and coarsely chopped
2 lb spinach, washed and trimmed
4 tablespoons butter
pinch of freshly grated nutmeg
salt and black pepper

Serves **4**
Prep time **10 minutes**
Cooking time **10 minutes**

AFFORDABILITY 1

POTATO WEDGES
WITH YOGURT & PARSLEY DIP (V)

1 Cut the potato into 8 wedges and cook them in a saucepan of lightly salted boiling water for 5 minutes. Drain the wedges thoroughly, then put them into a bowl with the red bell pepper slices and toss with the oil. Sprinkle with paprika and salt to taste.

2 Arrange the potato wedges and bell pepper slices on a baking sheet and cook under a preheated hot broiler for 6-8 minutes, turning occasionally, until cooked.

3 Meanwhile, for the yogurt and parsley dip, put the yogurt, parsley, scallions, and garlic, if using, into a bowl. Season to taste with salt and black pepper and mix thoroughly.

4 Serve the potato wedges and bell pepper slices hot with the yogurt dip.

1 large potato
1 red bell pepper, cored, seeded, and sliced
1 teaspoon olive oil
paprika, to taste
salt and black pepper

Yogurt and parsley dip
3 tablespoons plain yogurt
1 tablespoon chopped parsley
2 scallions, chopped
1 garlic clove, crushed (optional)

Serves **1**
Prep time **10 minutes**
Cooking time **15 minutes**

AFFORDABILITY
1

HEALTHY TIP

READ THE LABEL The term *low-fat* can be misleading and you shouldn't automatically assume that these are healthier options. Always read the ingredients list to check what the fat has been replaced with—often the sugar content will be bumped up to compensate.

Healthy MASHED POTATOES

1 Cook the potatoes in a large saucepan of lightly salted, boiling water for 15-20 minutes, until tender. Drain, reserving 2 tablespoons of the cooking water, and return the potatoes to the saucepan with the water.

2 Mash well until smooth. Stir in the sour cream and plenty of black pepper, then serve.

VARIATIONS

Mix and match any of the following ingredients, adding when mashing: finely grated zest of 1 lemon; a handful of finely chopped herbs, such as dill, parsley, chervil, tarragon, or chives; a couple of tablespoons of chopped (drained) capers or a small garlic clove, finely crushed. You can also use 3-4 tablespoons olive oil or milk instead of the sour cream, or swap half of the potatoes for a similar amount of parsnips, celeriac (celery root), or carrots, cooking them in the same pan as the potatoes.

4 russet potatoes, cut into chunks
¼ cup reduced-fat sour cream or
   plain Greek yogurt
salt and black pepper

Serves **2**
Prep time **10 minutes**
Cooking time **15-20 minutes**

AFFORDABILITY
1

ZUCCHINI & RICOTTA CUPS

1 Grease 8 cups of a muffin pan.

2 Use a vegetable peeler to make 16 long ribbons of zucchini and set aside. Shred the remaining zucchini and squeeze to remove any excess moisture. Mix the shredded zucchini with all the remaining ingredients in a bowl and season well with salt and black pepper.

3 Arrange 2 zucchini ribbons in a cross shape in each cup of the prepared muffin pan. Spoon in the filling and then fold over the overhanging zucchini ends. Bake in a preheated oven, at 375°F, for 15-20 minutes or until golden and cooked through. Turn out onto serving plates and serve immediately.

VARIATION

For mushrooms stuffed with zucchini and ricotta, brush a little olive oil over 4 large portobello mushrooms, trimmed, and place on a baking sheet, stem side up. Shred 1 zucchini and squeeze to remove any excess moisture, then mix with ³/₄ cup ricotta cheese, 4 drained and chopped sun-dried tomatoes in oil, and ¹/₄ cup chopped, pitted black ripe olives. Season with salt and black pepper, spoon onto the mushrooms, then sprinkle with ¹/₃ cup grated Parmesan-style cheese. Bake in a preheated oven, at 400°F, for 15 minutes, until golden and cooked through. Serve with ciabatta rolls.

butter, for greasing
2 zucchini
2 cups fresh white or whole wheat bread crumbs
1 cup ricotta cheese
1 cup grated Parmesan-style cheese
2 eggs, beaten
1 garlic clove, crushed
handful of chopped basil
salt and black pepper

Serves **4**
Prep time **15 minutes**
Cooking time **15-20 minutes**

AFFORDABILITY

FAST CHICKEN CURRY

PAN-COOKED EGGS
WITH SPINACH & LEEKS

LEBANESE TOMATO
& ZUCCHINI STEW

PUMPKIN & GOAT CHEESE CASSEROLE

Make it Light

ONE-DISH CHICKEN

AFFORDABILITY
1

1 Place the potatoes in a saucepan of boiling water and cook for 12–15 minutes, until tender. Drain, then cut into bite-size pieces.

2 Make a cut lengthwise down the side of each chicken breast to form a pocket, making sure that you do not cut all the way through. Mix together the herbs, garlic, and sour cream, season well with black pepper, then spoon a little of the mixture into each chicken pocket.

3 Put the leeks, endive, and potatoes into an ovenproof dish. Pour the broth over the vegetables, then lay the chicken breasts on top. Spoon the remaining sour cream mixture over the top, then bake in a preheated oven, at 400°F, for 25–30 minutes or until the chicken is cooked through. Serve immediately.

VARIATION

For baked chicken with fennel and potatoes, cut the cooked potatoes in half and put them into a large ovenproof dish with 1 large fennel bulb, cut into quarters. Omit the leeks and endive. Pour the broth over the vegetables and bake in a preheated oven, at 400°F, for 20 minutes. Remove from the oven and lay the u-filled chicken breasts over the vegetables. Combine 1 tablespoon chopped parsley with 1 tablespoon Dijon mustard and the reduced-fat sour cream, omitting the garlic, and spoon the mixture over the chicken. Bake for another 25–30 minutes, until the chicken is cooked through. Calories per serving 279

1 lb new potatoes
4 chicken breasts, about 4 oz each
⅓ cup chopped mixed herbs, such as parsley, chives, chervil, and mint
1 garlic clove, crushed
⅓ cup reduced-fat sour cream
8 baby leeks, trimmed and cleaned
2 endive heads, halved lengthwise
⅔ cup Chicken Broth (see page 244)
black pepper

Calories per serving **275**
Serves **4**
Prep time **10 minutes**
Cooking time **40–45 minutes**

SPICED ROASTED CHICKEN
with lime

1 Cut a few slashes across each chicken thigh. Mix together the harissa and honey and rub all over the chicken thighs. Put into a roasting pan large enough to spread everything out in a single layer, with the lime wedges, red bell pepper, zucchini, onion, and potatoes.

2 Drizzle with the oil, season with salt and black pepper, then roast in a preheated oven, at 425°F, for 25 minutes, turning occasionally, or until the chicken is cooked and the vegetables are tender. Serve with the juice of the lime wedges squeezed over the chicken.

VARIATION
For pan-fried spicy chicken, cut 8 small boneless, skinless chicken thighs into strips and coat in a mixture of 1 tablespoon harissa and 1 tablespoon honey. Heat 1 tablespoon sunflower oil in a large skillet, add the chicken, and cook over medium heat for 5 minutes. Add 1 cored, seeded, and chopped red bell pepper, 2 chopped zucchini, 1 onion, cut into thin wedges, and 2 limes, cut into wedges. Cook for 10 minutes, stirring occasionally, or until the chicken is cooked through and the vegetables are tender. Serve with new potatoes. Calories per serving 316

8 small (bone-in) chicken thighs, skinned
1 tablespoon harissa
¼ cup honey
2 limes, cut into wedges
1 red bell pepper, cored, seeded, and cut into large chunks
2 zucchini, cut into chunks
1 onion, cut into wedges
10 oz new potatoes, halved if large
1 tablespoon olive oil
salt and black pepper

Calories per serving **362**
Serves **4**
Prep time **15 minutes**
Cooking time **25 minutes**

Fast Chicken CURRY

AFFORDABILITY 2

1 Heat the oil in a nonstick saucepan over medium heat. Add the onion and cook for 3 minutes, until softened and translucent. Add the curry paste and cook, stirring, for 1 minute, until fragrant.

2 Add the chicken, tomatoes, broccoli, and coconut milk to the pan. Bring to a boil, then reduce the heat, cover, and simmer gently over low heat, stirring occasionally, for 15-20 minutes, until the chicken is cooked through.

3 Season well with salt and black pepper and serve immediately.

VARIATION
For chicken patties with curry sauce, follow the first stage of the recipe above, then add the tomatoes, 7 cups baby spinach leaves, and the reduced-fat coconut milk (omitting the chicken and broccoli), and cook as directed. Meanwhile, transfer 3 cups finely chopped, cooked boneless, skinless chicken breasts to a bowl and add 4 finely chopped scallions, 2 tablespoons chopped fresh cilantro, 1 cup fresh white or whole wheat bread crumbs, a squeeze of lemon juice, and 1 beaten egg. Season with salt and black pepper. Mix well, then form into 16 patties. Roll in 1/2 cup fresh white or whole wheat bread crumbs to coat. Brush a large skillet with a little vegetable oil and heat over medium heat. Add the patties, cooking in batches, and pan-fry on each side until golden brown and cooked through. Serve hot with the curry sauce. Calories per serving 490

3 tablespoons olive oil
1 onion, finely chopped
1/4 cup medium curry paste
8 boneless, skinless chicken thighs, cut into thin strips
1 (14 1/2 oz) can diced tomatoes
1/2 head of broccoli, broken into small florets, stems peeled and sliced
1/2 cup reduced-fat coconut milk
salt and black pepper

Calories per serving **413**
Serves **4**
Prep time **10 minutes**
Cooking time **20-25 minutes**

DEVILED CHICKEN

1   Remove the skin from the chicken thighs, open them out, and trim away any fat. Mix together the mustard, Tabasco, garlic, and soy sauce in a shallow dish.

2   Heat a large ridged grill pan or nonstick skillet until hot.

3   Dip the trimmed chicken thighs in the devil sauce and coat each piece well. Place the chicken pieces flat on the hot pan and cook for 8-10 minutes on each side. Serve hot or cold with a mixed leaf salad.

VARIATION
For jerk chicken, mix 3 tablespoons store-bought jerk marinade with the finely grated zest and juice of ½ orange and 2 finely chopped garlic cloves. Dip the chicken in this mixture then cook as above. Serve with Boiled Rice (see page 247) or a salad. Calories per serving 203

8 small-medium, boneless chicken thighs
2 tablespoons Dijon mustard
6 drops of Tabasco sauce
2 garlic cloves, crushed
1 tablespoon soy sauce
mixed leaf salad, to serve

Calories per serving **207**
Serves **4**
Prep time **10 minutes**
Cooking time **20 minutes**

LOW-FAT **LEMON CHICKEN**

1 Mix together the egg, garlic, and lemon zest in a shallow glass or ceramic dish. Add the chicken and toss to coat evenly, then cover and let marinate at room temperature for 10-15 minutes.

2 Discard the lemon zest, then add the cornstarch to the marinated chicken. Mix well to distribute the cornstarch evenly between the chicken slices.

3 Heat the oil in a nonstick wok or large skillet over high heat until the oil starts to shimmer. Add the chicken slices, making sure you leave a little space between them, and cook for 2 minutes on each side.

4 Reduce the heat to medium and stir-fry for another 1 minute or until the chicken is browned and cooked through. Increase the heat and pour in the lemon juice. Stir in the scallion, then garnish with lemon slices and serve immediately with boiled rice.

VARIATION
For warm lemon chicken and herb salad, cook the chicken as above, then toss in a bowl with ½ cucumber, sliced, a handful of fresh cilantro leaves, 6 torn basil leaves, and 2 cups argula. Dress the salad lightly with ½ teaspoon sesame oil and 1 teaspoon canola or olive oil. Calories per serving 263

1 egg, lightly beaten
2 garlic cloves, sliced
2 small pieces of lemon zest, plus the juice of 1 lemon
1 lb skinless chicken breasts, cut into ¼ inch slices
2 tablespoons cornstarch
1 tablespoon canola or olive oil
1 scallion, diagonally sliced into ¾ inch lengths
lemon slices, to garnish
Boiled Rice (see page 247), to serve

Calories per serving **417**
Serves **4**
Prep time **15 minutes, plus marinating**
Cooking time **8 minutes**

AFFORDABILITY 2

Chicken
WITH ORANGE & MINT

1 Season the chicken breasts with salt and black pepper. Heat the oil in a large nonstick skillet, add the chicken breasts, and cook over medium heat, turning once, for 4–5 minutes or until golden all over.

2 Pour in the orange juice, add the orange slices, then bring to a gentle simmer. Cover tightly, reduce the heat to low, and cook gently for 8–10 minutes or until the chicken is cooked through. Add the mint and butter and stir to mix well. Cook over high heat, stirring, for 2 minutes. Serve with steamed couscous, if desired.

VARIATION
For chicken with rosemary and lemon, bruise 4 sprigs of rosemary using a mortar and pestle, then chop finely. Put the grated zest and juice of 2 lemons, 3 crushed garlic cloves, ¼ cup olive oil, and the rosemary in a nonmetallic dish. Add the chicken breasts and mix to coat thoroughly. Cover and let marinate in the refrigerator for at least 30 mins or overnight. Cook the chicken breasts in a preheated hot ridged grill pan for 5 minutes on each side or until cooked through. Calories per serving 370

4 boneless, skinless chicken
  breasts, about 7 oz each
3 tablespoons olive oil
⅔ cup freshly squeezed orange
  juice
1 small orange, sliced
2 tablespoons chopped mint
1 tablespoon butter
salt and black pepper
steamed couscous, to serve
  (optional)

Calories per serving **355**
(excluding couscous)
Serves **4**
Prep time **5 minutes**
Cooking time **15-20 minutes**

LIVER WITH GARLICKY
mashed potatoes

1. Cook the potatoes and garlic in a saucepan of lightly salted boiling water for 10–12 minutes, until tender, then drain. Return the potatoes and garlic to the pan and mash with the sour cream and sage. Season well with black pepper.

2. Meanwhile, press the pieces of liver into the seasoned flour to coat them all over. Heat the oil in a nonstick skillet until hot, add the liver, and cook for 1–2 minutes on each side or until cooked to your preference. Serve with the garlic mashed potatoes and gravy.

3 russet potatoes, cubed
1 garlic clove, peeled
3 tablespoons reduced-fat sour cream
1½ teaspoons chopped sage
10 oz calf liver pieces
1 tablespoon all-purpose flour, seasoned with salt and black pepper
1½ teaspoons olive oil
salt and black pepper
Gravy (see page 245), to serve

Calories per serving **393**
Serves **2**
Prep time **10 minutes**
Cooking time **12–16 minutes**

BEEF
IN BLACK BEAN SAUCE

AFFORDABILITY 2

1 Heat 1 tablespoon of the oil in a nonstick wok over high heat until the oil starts to shimmer. Add half of the beef, season with salt, and stir-fry for 2 minutes. When it begins to brown, lift the beef onto a plate using a slotted spoon. Heat another 1 tablespoon of the oil and stir-fry the rest of the beef in the same way.

2 Return the wok to the heat and wipe it clean with paper towels. Heat the remaining oil and add the red bell pepper, corn, chile, and shallots. Stir-fry for 2 minutes before adding the black bean sauce, water, and cornstarch paste.

3 Bring to a boil, stirring, then return the beef to the wok and stir-fry until the sauce thickens and coats the ingredients in a velvety glaze. Serve with boiled rice, if desired.

VARIATION
For jumbo shrimp with scallions and black bean sauce, replace the beef with 8 oz peeled raw jumbo shrimp. Replace the corn, green chile, and shallots with 3/4 cup bean sprouts, 1 red chile, seeded and cut into strips, and 3 scallions cut into 1/2 inch pieces, and cook as above. Calories per serving 171 (excluding rice)

3 tablespoons peanut oil
1 lb sirloin beef, cut into thin slices
1 red bell pepper, cored, seeded, and cut into strips
6 baby corn, cut in half lengthwise
1 green chile, seeded and cut into strips
3 shallots, cut into thin wedges
2 tablespoons black bean sauce
1/4 cup water
1 teaspoon cornstarch mixed to a paste with 1 tablespoon water
salt
Boiled Rice (see page 247), to serve (optional)

Calories per serving **294** **(excluding rice)**
Serves **4**
Prep time **15 minutes**
Cooking time **10 minutes**

LEAN
LASAGNE

1   To make the meat sauce, put the eggplants, onions, garlic, broth, and wine into a large saucepan. Cover, bring to a boil, then simmer briskly for 5 minutes. Remove the lid and cook for another 5 minutes or until the eggplants are tender and the liquid is absorbed, adding a little more broth, if necessary. Remove from the heat and let cool slightly, then puree in a blender or food processor.

2   Meanwhile, brown the ground beef in a nonstick skillet. Skim off any fat. Add the eggplant mixture and the tomatoes and season with black pepper. Simmer briskly, uncovered, stirring occasionally, for about 10 minutes, until thickened.

3   Make the cheese sauce. Beat the egg whites with the ricotta in a bowl, then beat in the milk and ¼ cup of the Parmesan. Season with black pepper.

4   Alternate layers of the meat sauce, lasagna noodles, and cheese sauce in a 1¾ quart ovenproof dish, starting with the meat sauce and finishing with the cheese sauce. Sprinkle the top with the remaining Parmesan. Bake in a preheated oven, at 350°F, for 30-40 minutes, until browned. Serve hot.

8 oz oven-ready lasagna noodles

Meat sauce
2 eggplants, peeled and diced
2 red onions, chopped
2 garlic cloves, crushed
1¼ cups Vegetable Broth
  (see page 244)
¼ cup red wine
1 lb ground round beef
2 (14½ oz) cans diced tomatoes
black pepper

Cheese sauce
3 egg whites
1 cup ricotta cheese
¾ cup milk
⅓ cup grated Parmesan cheese

Calories per serving **340**
Serves **8**
Prep time **30 minutes**
Cooking time **50-60 minutes**

BROILED SARDINES
WITH TABBOULEH

1 Cook the bulgur wheat in a small saucepan of boiling water for 5 minutes, then drain and refresh under cold running water. Drain again and put into a bowl.

2 Meanwhile, dry-fry the onion in a small, nonstick skillet for 5 minutes. Put the tomatoes into a heatproof bowl and pour over enough boiling water to cover, then let stand for about 1 minute. Drain, skin the tomatoes, then seed and finely chop the flesh.

3 Add the onion, tomatoes, lemon juice, and lemon zest to the bulgur wheat. Reserve 4 mint leaves, then chop the rest. Stir the chopped mint into the bulgur wheat mixture and season with salt and black pepper.

4 Open out each sardine and lay a mint leaf along the center. Spoon a little of the tabbouleh down the center and carefully fold each fillet back over. Cook the sardines under a preheated hot broiler for 5 minutes, then carefully turn them over and cook for another 5 minutes or until cooked through. Serve with the remaining tabbouleh (hot or cold), lemon wedges, and a few salad greens or herbs.

1 cup bulgur wheat
1 onion, finely chopped
2 ripe tomatoes
1 tablespoon lemon juice
1 teaspoon finely grated
  lemon zest
small handful of mint leaves
4 small sardines, gutted and
  boned
salt and black pepper

To serve
lemon wedges
salad or herb leaves

Calories per serving **209**
Serves **4**
Prep time **15 minutes**
Cooking time **15 minutes**

STEAMED GINGER FISH

AFFORDABILITY 2

1 Pat the fish dry with paper towels and season well with salt and white pepper. Place in a single layer on a heatproof plate that will fit inside a bamboo steamer and sprinkle evenly with the ginger, chile, and orange and lemon zests.

2 Place the plate in a steamer (preferably bamboo), cover, and steam over a wok or large saucepan of boiling water for 6-8 minutes, until the fish is just cooked through—the flesh should be opaque in the center and slightly flaking but still moist.

3 Remove the plate from the steamer and drain off any liquid that may have accumulated around the fish. Sprinkle the scallions over the fish, then drizzle with the soy sauce and sprinkle with the chopped cilantro. Serve with stir-fry vegetable rice (see Tip) or boiled rice and steamed Asian greens.

ACCOMPANIMENT TIP
For stir-fry vegetable rice, to serve as an accompaniment, spray a large nonstick wok or skillet with a low-calorie cooking spray and place over high heat until almost smoking. Add 3½ cups cooled, freshly cooked jasmine rice and stir-fry for 3 minutes. Add 1 (1 lb) package mixed prepared stir-fry vegetables and stir-fry for 5 minutes. Season well with salt and black pepper, then stir in 2 tablespoons light soy sauce and 4 thinly sliced scallions and stir-fry for another 2 minutes. Serve immediately. Calories per serving 256

4 thick-cut halibut or cod fillets, about 7 oz each
thumb-size piece of fresh ginger root, peeled and finely shredded
1 red chile, seeded and finely shredded
1 tablespoon finely grated orange zest
1 tablespoon finely grated lemon zest
2 scallions, finely shredded
2 tablespoons light soy sauce
1 tablespoon finely chopped fresh cilantro leaves
salt and white pepper
Stir-fry Vegetable Rice (see Tip) or Boiled Rice (see page 247) and steamed Asian greens, to serve

Calories per serving **179 (excluding rice)**
Serves **4**
Prep time **15 minutes**
Cooking time **6-8 minutes**

CHILE & CILANTRO
FISH PACKAGE

AFFORDABILITY
1

1   Put the fish into a nonmetallic dish and sprinkle with the lemon juice. Cover and let marinate in the refrigerator for 15-20 minutes.

2   Put the cilantro, garlic, and chile into a mini food processor and process until the mixture forms a paste. Add the sugar and yogurt and briefly process to combine.

3   Lay the fish fillet on a sheet of nonstick parchment paper or aluminum foil and coat both sides with the paste. Gather up the paper or foil loosely around the fish and fold over at the top to seal. Chill in the refrigerator for at least 1 hour.

4   Place the package on a baking sheet and bake in a preheated oven, at 400°F, for about 15 minutes or until the fish is just cooked through. Serve garnished with extra cilantro and chile.

4 oz cod, halibut, or red snapper fillet
2 teaspoons lemon juice
1 tablespoon chopped fresh cilantro leaves, plus extra to garnish
1 garlic clove, peeled
1 green chile, seeded and chopped, plus extra to garnish
¼ teaspoon sugar
2 teaspoons plain yogurt

Calories per serving **127**
Serves **1**
Prep time **15 minutes, plus marinating and chilling**
Cooking time **15 minutes**

SQUID, PEPPER & RED RICE
PILAF

1 Slice the squid into rings. Toast the almonds in a dry skillet and slide out onto a plate. Heat the oil in the pan and gently cook the green bell peppers for 5 minutes to soften. Push the bell peppers to one side of the pan, add the squid rings, and cook for 3 minutes, until plumped up. Transfer the squid to a plate and set aside, leaving the bell peppers in the pan.

2 Add the onion and celery to the pan and cook for another 5 minutes, until all the vegetables start to brown. Add the garlic and cook for 1 minute.

3 Stir in the rice and broth. Cook gently, stirring frequently, for about 25 minutes, or according to the package directions, until the rice is tender. Add more hot water if the liquid has evaporated before the rice is tender.

4 Return the squid to the pan with the cilantro and heat through gently for 2 minutes or until the squid is hot. Season to taste with salt and black pepper and serve.

8 oz squid tubes
¼ cup slivered almonds
1 tablespoon olive oil
2 green bell peppers, cored, seeded, and coarsely chopped
1 red onion, thinly sliced
2 celery sticks, chopped
2 garlic cloves, crushed
¾ cup red rice or long-grain brown rice
2½ cups Vegetable or Chicken Broth (see pages 244)
2 tablespoons chopped fresh cilantro
salt and black pepper

Calories per serving **364**
Serves **2**
Prep time **15 minutes**
Cooking time **45 minutes**

AFFORDABILITY 2

KERALAN-STYLE MUSSELS

1 Scrub the mussels, scraping off any barnacles and pulling away the beards. Discard any damaged shells or open ones that do not close when tapped firmly against the side of the sink.

2 Melt the butter in a large saucepan and gently sauté the onion for 2 minutes. Add the garlic, cardamom pods, tamarind paste, and curry leaves and cook for 30 seconds. Add the tomatoes and broth and bring to a boil.

3 Add the mussels and cover with a lid. Cook for about 5 minutes, shaking the pan frequently until the shells have opened. Using a slotted spoon, drain the mussels to serving dishes (discarding any unopened mussels) and keep warm.

4 Add the coconut to the pan and heat through until almost boiling. Season to taste with salt and black pepper, then spoon the sauce over the mussels to serve. Serve with warm crusty bread.

2 lb fresh mussels
1 tablespoon butter
1 onion, finely chopped
3 garlic cloves, crushed
10 cardamom pods, crushed
1 teaspoon tamarind paste
6 curry leaves
2 tomatoes, skinned, seeded, and chopped
½ cup fish broth or Vegetable Broth (see page 244)
⅔ cup coconut milk
salt and black pepper
warm crusty bread, to serve

Calories per serving **446**
Serves **2**
Prep time **20 minutes**
Cooking time **10 minutes**

AFFORDABILITY
2

STIR-FRIED TOFU
WITH BASIL & CHILE

Vegan

1. Heat half of the oil in a nonstick wok or deep skillet until smoking, then add the tofu and stir-fry for 2-3 minutes, until golden all over. Remove to a plate with a slotted spoon.

2. Add the remaining oil to the pan with the ginger and garlic and stir-fry for 10 seconds, then add the broccoli and sugar snap peas and stir-fry for 1 minute.

3. Return the tofu to the pan and then add the broth, chili sauce, soy sauces, lime juice, and sugar. Stir-fry for 1 minute, until the vegetables are cooked but still crisp. Add the basil leaves, stir well, then serve.

VARIATION
For tofu and vegetables in oyster sauce, cook the tofu and vegetables as above. Return the tofu to the pan and add ¼ cup water, cook for 1 minute, then add ⅓ cup oyster sauce and heat through for another 1 minute. Omit the basil and garnish with chopped fresh cilantro. Calories per serving 244

2 tablespoons sunflower oil
12 oz firm tofu, drained and cubed
2 inch piece of fresh ginger root, peeled and grated
2 garlic cloves, chopped
½ head of broccoli, trimmed
4 cups trimmed sugar snap peas
⅔ cup Vegetable Broth (see page 244)
2 tablespoons sweet chili sauce
1 tablespoon light soy sauce
1 tablespoon dark soy sauce
1 tablespoon lime juice
2 teaspoons packed light brown sugar
handful of Thai basil leaves

Calories per serving **273**
Serves **4**
Prep time **20 minutes**
Cooking time **10 minutes**

Takeout Alternatives

There's nothing as satisfying as settling down to a night in front of the TV with a takeout being delivered to your front door. With pretty much every cuisine now just a phone call or mouse click away, you can indulge your cravings for everything from a pizza to a burger without having to lift a finger in the kitchen. However, while you might enjoy digging into a takeout, it will have a serious impact on your waistline and wallet.

Part of the appeal of dialing in an order for dinner is that you don't have to cook, but it's worth considering the fact that for the price of your chicken nuggets and sides, you could rustle up an equivalent feast for your whole household. So, here are some quick and easy alternatives to popular takeout treats.

FISH AND CHIPS

Homemade oven fries are just as tasty as those from your local fast food restaurant, and if you cut out the batter from the fish by broiling a piece of cod or halibut, you've turned a fat-charged Friday dinner into something more amenable to a healthy lifestyle. Don't forget to keep frozen peas in the freezer to add a quickly cooked side of peas.

THAI CURRY

You'll need an authentic red or green curry paste to make this rival the real thing. Cook chopped onion and strips of boneless, skinless chicken thigh meat until browned, stir in the curry paste, add the required amount of coconut milk, and stir until the chicken is cooked through. Serve with sticky or jasmine rice.

EGG-FRIED RICE

Cook the amount of rice you require and drain, then heat a little oil in a large saucepan. Sauté some chopped onion and add mushrooms, frozen (defrosted) peas, grated ginger, and garlic, if desired. Whisk a couple of eggs and pour into the pan, then use the spatula to break them up as they cook. Add the rice to the pan, stir until all the ingredients are combined, then serve.

KEBABS

This quick, healthy Middle Eastern-inspired alternative to a takeout burger, will be a hit with your pals. Thread diced boneless, skinless chicken breast (or thigh meat) and cored, seeded chunks of red bell pepper onto presoaked wooden skewers and broil until cooked through. Meanwhile, warm some pita breads, load them with shredded lettuce and hummus, and pile the chicken and bell peppers on top.

PIZZA

You can use store-bought pizza crusts or better still make your own dough. Alternatively, flatbreads, tortillas, and English muffins all make great bases. Spread over a layer of tomato puree or sauce, then add shredded cheese and other toppings of your choice, such as sliced bell pepper, red chile, cooked chicken, mushrooms, lean ham, etc. Cook in a hot oven for 5–8 minutes— it's literally that simple.

SPINACH & PEA FRITTATA

1 Heat the oil in a heavy, nonstick, ovenproof 9 inch skillet over low heat. Add the onion and cook, stirring occasionally, for 6–8 minutes, until softened, then stir in the spinach and peas and cook for another 2 minutes or until any moisture released by the spinach has evaporated.

2 Beat the eggs in a bowl and season lightly with salt and black pepper. Stir in the cooked vegetables, then pour the mixture back into the skillet and quickly arrange the vegetables so that they are evenly dispersed. Cook over low heat for 8–10 minutes or until all but the top of the frittata is set.

3 Transfer the skillet to a preheated hot broiler and cook about 4 inches from the heat source until the top is set but not browned. Give the pan a shake to loosen the frittata, then transfer to a plate to cool. Serve slightly warm or at room temperature, accompanied by a green salad, if desired.

VARIATION
For a zucchini, pea, and cheese frittata, follow the first step as above, but replace the spinach with 1 large zucchini, shredded. Add ¼ cup grated Parmesan-style cheese and 1 cup cubed mozzarella cheese to the raw egg mixture with the vegetables and cook as above. Calories per serving 312

1 tablespoon olive oil
1 onion, thinly sliced
5 cups baby spinach leaves
1 cup shelled fresh or frozen peas
6 eggs
salt and black pepper
green salad, to serve (optional)

Calories per serving **201**
(excluding green salad)
Serves **4**
Prep time **10 minutes,**
plus cooling
Cooking time **25 minutes**

AFFORDABILITY 1

Sweet Potato, Red Onion & Dill FRITTATA (V)

1. Heat the oil in a nonstick skillet about 8½ inches in diameter. Add the onions and sweet potatoes and sauté gently for 10-15 minutes, until softened and pale golden. Stir the vegetables frequently to prevent them from overbrowning.

2. Whisk the eggs in a bowl to break up. Beat in the dill and a little salt and black pepper.

3. Reduce the heat to its lowest setting and pour the eggs evenly over the vegetables in the pan. Cook gently for a couple of minutes, pushing the cooked egg mixture from the edges of the pan in toward the center. Once partly cooked, cover the pan with aluminum foil or a lid and cook for another 3-4 minutes or until the eggs are lightly set.

4. Let cool slightly, turn out onto a plate, and serve warm, or let cool completely before serving.

3 tablespoons olive oil
2 red onions, thinly sliced
3 sweet potatoes (about 1 lb), peeled and cut into ¾ inch chunks
5 eggs
3 tablespoons chopped dill
salt and black pepper

Calories per serving **636**
Serves **2**
Prep time **10 minutes, plus cooling**
Cooking time **20 minutes**

AFFORDABILITY 1

HEALTHY TIP

CUT DOWN ON CAFFEINE There's nothing wrong with the odd cup of coffee to get your through a tedious late-afternoon lecture. But if there's a caffeine hit in your hand every break, it's time to cut down. Try switching every other coffee for a peppermint or green tea.

PAN-COOKED EGGS
WITH SPINACH & LEEKS

1 Melt the butter in a skillet, add the leek and red pepper flakes, and cook over medium-high heat for 4-5 minutes, until softened. Add the spinach and season well with salt and black pepper, then toss and cook for 2 minutes, until the spinach has wilted.

2 Make 2 wells in the center of the vegetables and break an egg into each well. Cook over low heat for 2-3 minutes, until the eggs are set. Spoon the yogurt on top, sprinkle with the paprika, and serve.

2 tablespoons butter
1 leek, trimmed, cleaned, and thinly sliced
¼ teaspoon dried red pepper flakes
2 (5 oz) packages baby spinach
2 eggs
3 tablespoons plain yogurt
pinch of ground paprika
salt and black pepper

Calories per serving **265**
Serves **2**
Prep time **10 minutes**
Cooking time **10 minutes**

HEALTHY TIP

DRINK RESPONSIBLY When you reach the age of 21, it might be tempting to binge drink. However, if you want a clear head in the morning, it is best to alternate your regular beer with bottles of low alcohol or alcohol-free brands.

TOMATO & HERB PIZZA PIE (V)

1   Lightly grease a baking sheet and set aside.

2   Make the pie crust. Sift the flour and baking powder into a mixing bowl, tipping in the grain left in the sifter, then rub in the spread until the mixture resembles fine bread crumbs. Add just enough milk to make a soft dough. Turn out on to a lightly floured surface and knead until smooth. Roll out to a 9-10 inch diameter circle, then place on the prepared baking sheet.

3   For the topping, heat the oil in a large, nonstick saucepan, add the onion and garlic, and sauté gently for 5 minutes, until softened. Add the green or red bell pepper, tomatoes, tomato paste, and basil or thyme and simmer, uncovered, stirring occasionally, for about 10 minutes, until the mixture is thick. Season with black pepper.

4   Spread the tomato mixture over the pie crust to the edge. Top with the mozzarella cheese. Bake in a preheated oven, at 425°F, for 20-25 minutes, until the topping is bubbling. Garnish with basil sprigs and serve.

VARIATION

For the topping, you could instead try: anchovy fillets and black ripe olives; red onion, feta cheese, red bell pepper and arugula; spinach and ricotta.

¼ cup unsaturated spread,
   plus extra for greasing
2½ cups whole wheat flour,
   plus extra for dusting
2½ teaspoons baking powder
⅔ cup skim milk

Topping
1 tablespoon olive oil
2 large onions, chopped
1-2 garlic cloves, crushed
1 green or red bell pepper, cored,
   seeded, and sliced
2 (14½ oz) cans tomatoes
2 tablespoons tomato paste
large handful of basil or thyme,
   chopped
4 oz reduced-fat mozzarella
   cheese, sliced
bell pepper
basil sprigs, to garnish

Calories per serving **340**
Serves **6**
Prep time **15 minutes**
Cooking time **35-40 minutes**

AFFORDABILITY 1

HEALTHY TIP

Homemade pizzas can be healthy, with a starchy crust topped with your own choice of fresh vegetables and low-fat ingredients. Look for reduced-fat mozzarella cheese and avoid adding large quantities of meat toppings that are loaded with fat.

Five Veggie Pizza Ⓥ

AFFORDABILITY 1

1 Put the flour, yeast, salt, and oil into a bowl. Add the warm milk and water mixture and mix with a blunt knife to make a dough, adding a little more water if the dough feels dry and crumbly. Turn out onto a lightly floured surface and knead for 10 minutes, until the dough is smooth and elastic. Put in a lightly oiled bowl, cover with plastic wrap, and let rise in a warm place for about 45 minutes, until risen to about twice the size.

2 For the tomato sauce, put the tomatoes, tomato paste, and garlic into a small saucepan and cook for 5 minutes, until thickened.

3 Heat the oil in a nonstick skillet and sauté the fennel for 5 minutes, stirring. Add the zucchini and red bell pepper and sauté for 3 minutes, stirring. Add the spinach and turn with the cooked vegetables to lightly wilt. Season with salt and black pepper.

4 Roll out the dough on a lightly floured surface until about 12 inches in diameter. Spread evenly with the tomato sauce and then sprinkle with the vegetables, spreading them to the edges. Arrange the mozzarella slices on top and sprinkle with the Parmesan-style or Cheddar-style cheese.

5 Bake in a preheated oven, at 450°F, for 12 minutes or until the cheese is bubbling and golden. Serve with a mixed salad.

1¼ cups whole wheat bread flour, plus extra for dusting
1 teaspoon active dry yeast
½ teaspoon salt
2 tablespoons olive oil, plus extra for greasing
½ cup lukewarm mixed milk and water

Topping
¾ cup can diced tomatoes
2 tablespoons tomato paste
1 garlic clove, crushed
1 tablespoon olive oil
1 small fennel bulb, halved and thinly sliced
1 zucchini, thinly sliced
1 red bell pepper, cored, seeded, and sliced
2 cups spinach
4 oz mozzarella cheese, thinly sliced
½ cup grated Parmesan-style cheese or shredded cheddar-style cheese
salt and black pepper

mixed salad, to serve

Calories per serving **458**
Serves **3**
Prep time **25 minutes, plus rising**
Cooking time **25 minutes**

PUMPKIN
& GOAT CHEESE CASSEROLE (V)

1 Put the beets, pumpkin, and onion into a roasting pan, drizzle with the oil, and sprinkle with the fennel seeds and salt and black pepper. Roast the vegetables in a preheated oven, at 400°F, for 20-25 minutes, turning once, until well browned and tender.

2 Cut the goat cheeses in half and nestle each half among the roasted vegetables. Sprinkle the cheeses with a little salt and black pepper and drizzle with some of the pan juices.

3 Return the dish to the oven for about 5 minutes, until the cheese is just beginning to melt. Sprinkle with rosemary and serve immediately.

VARIATION
For penne with beets and pumpkin, roast the vegetables as above for 20-25 minutes, omitting the fennel seeds. Cook 12 oz penne pasta in a saucepan of lightly salted boiling water according to the package directions, then drain, reserving one ladleful of the cooking water. Return the pasta to the pan and add the roasted vegetables, a handful of torn basil leaves, and the cooking water. Omit the goat cheese and rosemary. Cook over high heat, stirring, for 30 seconds, then serve. Calories per serving 482

5 raw beets, peeled and diced
¼ pumpkin or ½ butternut squash, peeled, seeded, and cut into slightly larger dice
1 red onion, cut into wedges
2 tablespoons olive oil
2 teaspoons fennel seeds
2 small goat cheeses, about 3½ oz each
salt and black pepper
chopped rosemary, to garnish

Calories per serving **330**
Serves **4**
Prep time **20 minutes**
Cooking time **25-30 minutes**

Mushroom Stroganoff

1 Melt the butter with the oil in a large, nonstick skillet, add the onion and garlic, and sauté, stirring occasionally, until soft and starting to brown.

2 Add the mushrooms to the pan and cook, stirring occasionally, until soft and starting to brown. Stir in the mustard and sour cream and just heat through. Season to taste with salt and black pepper, then serve immediately, garnished with the chopped parsley.

VARIATION

For mushroom soup with garlic croutons, while the mushrooms are cooking, remove the crusts from 2 thick slices of day-old white bread and rub with 2 halved garlic cloves. Cut the bread into cubes. Fry the cubes of bread in a little vegetable oil in a nonstick skillet, turning constantly, for 5 minutes or until browned all over and crisp. Drain on paper towels. After adding the mustard and sour cream to the mushroom mixture as above, add 1²/₃ cups hot Vegetable Broth (see page 244), then puree the mixture in a blender or food processor until smooth. Serve in bowls, topped with the croutons and garnished with the chopped parsley. Calories per serving 273

1 tablespoon butter
2 tablespoons olive oil
1 onion, thinly sliced
4 garlic cloves, finely chopped
7 cups trimmed and sliced cremini mushrooms (about 1 lb)
2 tablespoons whole-grain mustard
1 cup reduced-fat sour cream
salt and black pepper
3 tablespoons chopped parsley, to garnish

Calories per serving **239**
Serves **4**
Prep time **10 minutes**
Cooking time **10 minutes**

LEBANESE TOMATO & ZUCCHINI STEW

Vegan

1. Heat the oil in a large, nonstick saucepan over low heat. Add the onion and sauté, stirring occasionally, for 10-12 minutes, until soft and translucent. Add the zucchini and cook for another 5-6 minutes, stirring occasionally.

2. Add the tomatoes (including the juice) and garlic and continue to cook over medium heat for another 20 minutes, stirring occasionally.

3. Stir in the chili powder, turmeric, and dried mint and cook for another few minutes to let the flavors mingle. Season to taste with salt and black pepper. Garnish with mint leaves and serve with boiled rice.

1 tablespoon light olive oil
1 large onion, finely chopped
4 zucchini, cut into ½ x 1½ inch sticks
2 (14½ oz) cans whole plum tomatoes
2 garlic cloves, crushed
½ teaspoon chili powder
¼ teaspoon ground turmeric
2 teaspoons dried mint
salt and black pepper
mint leaves, to garnish
1 cup Boiled Rice (see page 247) per person, to serve

Calories per serving **266**
Serves **4**
Prep time **10 minutes**
Cooking time **40-45 minutes**

AFFORDABILITY
1

Sweet Alternatives

TOFFEE & CHOCOLATE POPCORN

STRAWBERRY & ALMOND
LAYERED DESSERTS

CHOCOLATE, ZUCCHINI & NUT CAKE

ROASTED HONEY PEACHES

LEMON DRIZZLE CAKE

1 Grease and line the bottom and sides of an 8½ inch square cake pan with parchment paper.

2 Put the eggs, granulated sugar, and salt into a large, heatproof bowl set over a saucepan of barely simmering water and beat with a handheld electric mixer for 2–3 minutes or until the mixture triples in volume and thickens to the consistency of lightly whipped cream. Remove from the heat. Sift in the flour and baking powder, add the lemon zest and juice, and drizzle the butter down the side of the bowl. Fold in gently.

3 Pour the batter into the prepared pan. Bake in a preheated oven, at 350°F, for 20–25 minutes or until risen, golden, and coming away from the sides of the pan.

4 Meanwhile, put all the syrup ingredients into a small saucepan and heat gently until the sugar dissolves, stirring. Increase the heat and boil rapidly, without stirring, for 4–5 minutes. Set aside to cool a little.

5 Let the cake to cool in the pan for 5 minutes, then make holes over the surface with a toothpick. Drizzle two-thirds of the warm syrup (reserve the rest) over the top of the cake. Let the cake cool completely in the pan and absorb the syrup.

6 Turn the cake out of the pan and peel off the lining paper. Cut into squares or slices and serve each portion with about 1 heaping teaspoon of reduce-fat crème fraîche or Greek yogurt and an extra drizzle of the remaining syrup.

VARIATION

For citrus drizzle cake with sorbet, make the cake as above, replacing the lemon zest and juice with the finely grated zest of 1 orange and 1 tablespoon orange juice. Serve topped with lemon sorbet.

1 stick (4 oz) butter, melted and
    cooled, plus extra for greasing
5 eggs
½ cup granulated sugar
pinch of salt
1 cup all-purpose flour
1 teaspoon baking powder
finely grated zest of 1 lemon
1 tablespoon lemon juice

Syrup

2 cups confectioners' sugar, sifted
½ cup lemon juice
finely grated zest of 1 lemon
seeds scraped from 1 vanilla bean

reduced-fat crème fraîche or
    Greek yogurt, to serve

Serves **8**
Prep time **20 minutes,**
plus cooling
Cooking time **22–28 minutes**

AFFORDABILITY 2

ZUCCHINI, LEMON & POPPY SEED CAKE

(V)

1 Grease and line the sides and bottom of an 8½ x 4½ inch loaf pan with parchment paper.

2 Sift the flour and baking powder into a bowl. Beat the eggs in a separate mixing bowl with the oil, honey, sugar, poppy seeds, and lemon zest and juice. Stir in the shredded zucchini. Add the flour and stir gently to mix.

3 Transfer the batter to the prepared pan and level the surface. Bake in a preheated oven, at 325°F, for 40-45 minutes or until risen and just firm to the touch. A toothpick inserted into the center should come out clean. Transfer to a wire rack to cool.

4 For the frosting, spoon the yogurt onto several sheets of paper towels. Place several more sheets on top and press firmly to squeeze out as much liquid as possible. Turn the yogurt into a bowl and stir in the lemon curd. Spread over the top of the cold cake. Serve in slices.

⅓ cup olive oil, plus extra for greasing
1⅓ cups spelt flour
1 teaspoon baking powder
2 eggs
¼ cup honey
¼ cup granulated sugar
2 tablespoons poppy seeds
finely grated zest and juice of 1 lemon
1 cup shredded zucchini

Frosting
½ cup nonfat Greek yogurt
2 tablespoons lemon curd

Serves **8**
Prep time **15 minutes, plus cooling**
Cooking time **45 minutes**

GF V

BERRY-TOPPED
CORNMEAL MUG CAKE

1 Beat together the cornmeal, butter, honey, and almond meal in a 1 cup microwave-proof mug. Add the egg and beat together until well mixed. Microwave on full power for 1 minute.

2 Spoon the berries and preserves on top and stir in lightly so the cornmeal mixture is marbled with the fruit. Microwave on full power for 1 minute. Serve drizzled with extra honey.

2 tablespoons cornmeal
2 tablespoons salted butter, softened
2 tablespoons honey, plus extra to drizzle
2 tablespoons almond meal (ground almonds)
1 egg
2 tablespoons black currants or blueberries
1 tablespoon black currant or blueberry preserves

Serves **1**
Prep time **5 minutes**
Cooking time **2 minutes**

AFFORDABILITY
1

SPICED PASSION MUG CAKE

1 Put the honey, butter, egg, flour, baking powder, and ginger into a 1½ cup microwave-proof mug and beat together until well mixed. Add the carrot and pineapple and mix well.

2 Microwave on full power for 2 minutes or until just firm to touch and a toothpick inserted into the center comes out clean. Serve topped with the cream cheese and drizzled with the ginger syrup.

2 tablespoons honey
2 tablespoons salted butter, softened
1 egg
3 tablespoons all-purpose flour
¼ teaspoon baking powder
1 inch piece of preserved ginger in syrup, drained and chopped
2 inch piece of carrot, finely grated
½ fresh or canned pineapple slice, chopped
1 tablespoon cream cheese
1 tablespoon preserved ginger syrup, to drizzle

Serves **1**
Prep time **5 minutes**
Cooking time **2 minutes**

AFFORDABILITY **1**

Chocolate, ZUCCHINI & NUT CAKE

(V)

1. Grease and line the bottom an 8 inch, round, deep, loose-bottom cake pan with parchment paper.

2. Place the zucchini into a strainer and squeeze out any excess liquid. Beat together the eggs, oil, orange zest and juice, and sugar in a large bowl. Sift in the flour, cocoa powder, baking soda, and baking powder and beat to combine. Fold in the zucchini and apricots, then spoon the batter into the prepared pan and level the surface.

3. Bake in a preheated oven, at 350°F, for 40 minutes, until risen and firm to the touch. Let cool in the pan for 5 minutes. Turn out onto a wire rack and let cool completely.

4. For the topping, beat together the cream cheese and chocolate hazelnut spread in a bowl, then spread it over the top of the cake. Sprinkle with the chopped hazelnuts. Serve in slices.

½ cup vegetable oil, plus extra for greasing
2 cups shredded zucchini
2 eggs
finely grated zest and juice of 1 orange
⅔ cup granulated sugar
1¾ cups all-purpose flour
2 tablespoons unsweetened cocoa powder
½ teaspoon baking soda
2¼ teaspoons baking powder
⅓ cup chopped dried apricots

Topping
1 cup cream cheese
2 tablespoons vegetarian-friendly chocolate hazelnut spread
1 tablespoon hazelnuts, toasted and chopped

Serves **12**
Prep time **20 minutes, plus cooling**
Cooking time **40 minutes**

AFFORDABILITY 2

GLUTEN-FREE
COCONUT & MANGO CAKE Ⓥ

THIS DELICIOUS TROPICAL-INSPIRED CAKE IS GREAT FOR SUMMER
EATING WITH A BUNCH OF FRIENDS.

1 Grease and line the bottom of a 9 inch round, deep, loose-bottom cake pan with parchment paper.

2 Put the butter and brown sugar into a large bowl and beat together until light and fluffy, then beat in the egg yolks, buttermilk, cornmeal, rice flour, baking powder, coconut milk powder, and dried coconut. Whisk the egg whites in a separate large, clean bowl until they form soft peaks, then fold into the cake mixture with the pureed mango.

3 Spoon the batter into the prepared pan, level the surface, then bake in a preheated oven, at 400°F, for 45-50 minutes, until golden and firm to the touch. Let cool in the pan for 5 minutes. Transfer to a wire rack to cool completely.

4 When the cake is cold, slice it in half horizontally. Place the filling ingredients in a bowl and mix together until combined. Use half of the filling to sandwich the cake together, then spread the remaining mixture over the top. Serve in slices.

1 stick (4 oz) butter, softened,
  plus extra for greasing
½ cup packed light brown sugar
4 eggs, separated
1²⁄₃ cups buttermilk
1½ cups cornmeal
1⅓ cups rice flour
2 teaspoons gluten-free
  baking powder
½ cup coconut milk powder
¾ cup unsweetened dried coconut
1 ripe mango, peeled, pitted, and
  flesh pureed

Filling
1 cup mascarpone cheese
1 ripe mango, peeled, pitted, and
  finely chopped
2 tablespoons confectioners'
  sugar

Serves **12**
Prep time **20 minutes,**
plus cooling
Cooking time **45-50 minutes**

AFFORDABILITY
3

EASY ALMOND MACARONS

1   Line a large baking sheet with nonstick parchment paper.

2   Whisk the egg whites in a clean bowl with a handheld electric mixer until soft peaks form. Gradually whisk in the sugar, a spoonful at a time, until thick and glossy. Fold in the almond meal until combined.

3   Drop tablespoonfuls of the paste, slightly apart, onto the prepared baking sheet. Press an almond on top of each.

4   Bake in a preheated oven, at 350°F, for about 15 minutes, until the macarons are pale golden and just crisp. Let rest on the paper to cool for 5 minutes, then transfer to a wire rack to cool completely before serving.

VARIATION

For scribbled chocolate macarons, make the macarons as above, replacing ¼ cup of the almond meal with ¼ cup unsweetened cocoa powder and omitting the whole almonds. Heat 2 oz semisweet or milk chocolate, evenly chopped, in a microwave-proof mug in a microwave in two or three 30 second bursts, stirring inbetween, until almost melted (it will continue to melt), then drizzle it over the cooled macarons with a teaspoon. Let the chocolate set before serving.

2 egg whites
½ cup superfine sugar (or grind
   ½ cup granulated sugar in a
   food processor for 1 minute)
1 almond meal (ground almonds)
blanched whole almonds, to
   decorate

Makes about **15**
Prep time **15 minutes,**
plus cooling
Cooking time **15 minutes**

CHOCOLATE PEANUT COOKIES  Ⓥ

1   Line a large baking sheet with nonstick parchment paper.

2   Combine the flour, baking soda, and sugar in a bowl. Add the peanut butter, honey, oil, and chocolate and mix to form a thick dough.

3   Take spoonfuls of the dough and roll between the palms of your hands into a ball, each about the size of a whole walnut. Space well apart on the prepared baking sheet.

4   Bake in a preheated oven, at 375°F, for 10 minutes, until the cookies have risen and turned golden. Let rest on the baking sheet for 2 minutes, until firm, then transfer to a wire rack to cool.

2/3 cup rice flour
1 teaspoon baking soda
¼ cup packed light brown sugar
¾ cup chunky peanut butter
¼ cup honey
2 tablespoons mild olive oil
    or vegetable oil
3 oz semisweet chocolate,
    chopped

Makes **20**
Prep time **10 minutes,
plus cooling**
Cooking time **10 minutes**

AFFORDABILITY
2

BUG BUSTING

Unfortunately, student living goes hand in hand with getting sick. Living in close proximity to other people harboring a bunch of germs, combined with burning the candle at both ends, is a sure-fire way to end up sick in bed. Common coughs and colds, the dreaded flu, and other contagious illnesses are all part and package of leaving home. But there are certain steps you can take to minimize your chances of drowning in a cold sweat in your room without your mom to mop your brow.

SLEEP

It's tempting to forget about your shut-eye time while you try to keep up with work and a packed social life, but a lack of sleep can lead to being run down and more prone to infections. Sleep deprivation can have a big impact on your immune system and you'll be more probable to pick up illnesses as well as take longer to recover; ideally, you should get 7–9 hours of sleep a night.

DON'T STRESS OUT

The stereotype of the lazy student is seriously outdated and it's stress that we need to worry about these days. With the pressure piled on for essays and exams, and working and living independently, it's no surprise that students feel strung out. But stress can have an adverse effect on your health and lead to illness, so it's important to manage stress before it takes over your life.

HYGIENE

Germs love nothing more than poor hygiene, so don't encourage them—wash your hands with antibacterial soap, keep bathrooms and kitchens clean, and be extra careful with food prep. It also makes sense to steer clear of your buddies when they're harboring an unpleasant illness.

EXERCISE

Regular exercise can help to build a healthy immune system by promoting good circulation.

HEALTHY EATING

It goes without saying that a balanced, healthy diet will boost your body's natural defenses against viruses and will help you to fight infection if you do become sick.

CRANBERRY & HAZELNUT COOKIES (V)

1 Line 2 large baking sheets with wax or parchment paper.

2 Beat together the butter, sugars, egg, and vanilla extract in a large bowl until smooth. Stir in the flour and oats, then the cranberries and hazelnuts.

3 Place teaspoonfuls of the dough onto the prepared baking sheets, leaving space between each one, then flatten them slightly with the back of a fork.

4 Bake in a preheated oven, at 350°F, for 5-6 minutes, until lightly browned. Let cool for 2-3 minutes. Transfer to a wire rack and let cool completely.

VARIATION
For semisweet chocolate and ginger cookies, prepare the dough as above, omitting the dried cranberries and hazelnuts. Replace them with ¼ cup semisweet chocolate chips or chunks and 2 pieces of drained, chopped preserved ginger (or ½ teaspoon peeled and grated fresh ginger root). Stir together, then bake and cool as above.

4 tablespoons unsalted butter, softened
3 tablespoons granulated sugar
2 tablespoons packed light brown sugar
1 egg, beaten
few drops of vanilla extract
1¼ cups all-purpose flour, sifted
1¼ teaspoons baking powder
½ cup rolled oats
⅓ cup dried cranberries
⅓ cup hazelnuts, toasted and chopped

Makes **30**
Prep time **10 minutes, plus cooling**
Cooking time **6 minutes**

TOFFEE & CHOCOLATE POPCORN Ⓥ

1 Put the popping corn into a large bowl. Cover the bowl with a vented food cover (or wax paper with slits cut into it, held in place with a rubber band). Microwave on full power for 4 minutes. Alternatively, cook in a saucepan with a lid on the stove over medium heat for a few minutes, shaking the pan occasionally to avoid burning the kernels, until the rapid popping slows down to a few pops, then remove from the heat and let stand until the popping stops completely.

2 Meanwhile, gently heat the butter, brown sugar, and cocoa powder together in a saucepan, stirring until the sugar has dissolved and the butter has melted. Stir the warm popcorn into the mixture and serve.

VARIATION
For toffee, marshmallow, and nut popcorn, omit the brown sugar and cocoa powder. Microwave the popping corn as above, then gently heat 5 oz chewy toffees, 1 stick (4 oz) butter, 16 marshmallows, and 2 oz semisweet chocolate, chopped, in a saucepan until melted and combined. Serve as above.

½ cup popping corn
2 sticks (8 oz) butter
2¼ cups packed light brown sugar
2 tablespoons unsweetened cocoa powder

Serves **12 as a snack**
Prep time **1 minutes**
Cooking time **4 minutes**

MANGO & PASSION FRUIT
TRIFLE Ⓥ

1 Break each ladyfinger into 4 pieces and divide between
2 glasses. Mix the yogurt and crème fraîche together
in a bowl.

2 Halve the passion fruit and scoop out the pulpy seeds.
Spoon two-thirds of the seeds over the ladyfingers, then
add half of the mango pieces.

3 Spoon half of the yogurt mixture over the fruit, then top with
the remaining mango. Spoon the remaining yogurt mixture
over the top and finish with the remaining passion fruit
seeds. Chill in the refrigerator for 1 hour before serving.

2 ladyfingers
⅓ cup nonfat Greek yogurt
½ cup reduced-fat crème fraîche
  or mascarpone cheese
2 passion fruit
½ ripe mango, peeled, pitted,
  and diced

Serves **2**
Prep time **15 minutes,
plus chilling**

AFFORDABILITY
2

BAKED STRAWBERRIES & MERINGUE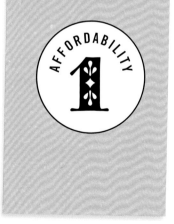

1 Line 4 individual tart pans or ramekins with nonstick parchment paper.

2 Whisk the egg whites in a bowl until they form stiff peaks, then beat in the sugar, a spoonful at a time, making sure the sugar is incorporated between additions. Fold in the cornstarch, vinegar, and vanilla extract until combined.

3 Spoon the mixture into the prepared tart pans or ramekins and cook in a preheated oven, at 250°F, for 2½ hours. Place the strawberries in an ovenproof dish and bake with the meringues for the last hour of the cooking time.

4 Spoon the baked strawberries and any cooking juices over the meringues to serve.

VARIATION

For baked nectarines with orange meringues, add the finely grated zest of 1 orange to the meringue mixture with the cornstarch. Cut 2 peeled and pitted nectarines into thin slices and put into an ovenproof dish. Sprinkle with 2 tablespoons sugar and 1 tablespoon orange juice, then bake for 45 minutes with the meringues. Serve the fruit over the meringues.

3 egg whites
¾ cup packed light brown sugar
1 tablespoon cornstarch
1 teaspoon distilled white vinegar
1 teaspoon vanilla extract
1⅔ cups hulled and sliced
  strawberries

Serves **4**
Prep time **15 minutes**
Cooking time **2½ hours**

AFFORDABILITY
1

ROASTED HONEY PEACHES

1 Spoon the honey into a small saucepan. Scrape the seeds from the vanilla bean and add the seeds and bean to the pan. Heat gently, stirring occasionally for 1-2 minutes. Stir in the sesame seeds.

2 Place the peaches, cut side down, in a roasting pan and pour the honey mixture over them. Bake in a preheated oven, at 350°F, for 20-25 minutes, until the peaches are soft. Baste a couple of times with the juices during cooking.

3 Serve the baked peaches warm with vanilla ice cream or yogurt, if desired.

2 tablespoons orange blossom honey
1 vanilla bean, halved lengthwise
2-3 teaspoons sesame seeds
4 peaches, halved and pitted
vanilla ice cream or reduced-fat Greek yogurt, to serve (optional)

Serves **4**
Prep time **10 minutes**
Cooking time **25-30 minutes**

AFFORDABILITY
1

BERRY & MINT COMPOTE

1 Put the fruit, cinnamon stick, and orange zest and juice into a small saucepan and simmer gently for 12–15 minutes.

2 Remove the cinnamon stick and let the compote cool for 3–4 minutes, then stir in the mint.

3 Serve with dollops of plain yogurt, if desired.

4 cups mixed fruit, such as strawberries, blackberries, raspberries, and halved and pitted plums
1 cinnamon stick
finely grated zest and juice of 1 orange
8 mint leaves, shredded
plain yogurt, to serve (optional)

Serves **4**
Prep time **10 minutes, plus cooling**
Cooking time **15 minutes**

AFFORDABILITY 1

Instant
APPLE CRISPS

6 cooking apples (about 2 lb),
  such as Granny Smiths, peeled,
  cored, and thickly sliced
2 tablespoons butter
2 tablespoons granulated sugar
1 tablespoon lemon juice
2 tablespoons water

Crumb topping
4 tablespoons butter
1½ cups fresh whole wheat
  bread crumbs
3 tablespoons pumpkin seeds
2 tablespoons packed brown sugar

Serves **4**
Prep time **10 minutes**
Cooking time **13 minutes**

1 Put the apples into a saucepan with the butter, granulated sugar, lemon juice, and water. Cover and simmer for 8–10 minutes, until softened. Remove from the heat.

2 For the crumb topping, melt the butter in a skillet, add the bread crumbs, and cook over medium heat until light golden, then add the pumpkin seeds and cook for another 1 minute. Remove from the heat and stir in the brown sugar.

3 Spoon the apple mixture into bowls, sprinkle with the crumb topping, and serve.

VARIATION
For instant pear and chocolate crips, peel, core, and slice 6 pears (about 2 lb) and cook them with the butter, granulated sugar, and water as above, adding ½ teaspoon ground ginger instead of the lemon juice. Prepare the crumb topping as above, replacing the pumpkin seeds with 2 oz semisweet chocolate, coarsely chopped. Cook and serve as above.

AFFORDABILITY
1

STRAWBERRY & ALMOND LAYERED DESSERTS Ⓥ

1 Place the slivered almonds and coconut on a baking sheet and cook under a preheated medium-hot broiler for 3-4 minutes, until golden. Give the sheet a little shake at least once to make sure the almonds are lightly toasted on both sides. Let cool.

2 Spoon half of the almond and coconut mixture into 4 glasses. Top with half of the sliced strawberries, then all of the yogurt.

3 Top with the remaining strawberries, then the remaining almond and coconut mixture. Spoon the honey over the top and serve.

¼ cup slivered almonds
¼ cup unsweetened dried coconut
2 cups hulled and sliced strawberries
1 cup plain yogurt
4 teaspoons honey

Serves **4**
Prep time **10 minutes, plus cooling**
Cooking time **3-4 minutes**

AFFORDABILITY
1

LEMON & GOLDEN RAISIN RICE PUDDING

1 Scrape the seeds from the vanilla bean and add the seeds and bean to a saucepan with the rice, milk, golden raisins, and lemon zest.

2 Bring to a boil, then reduce the heat and simmer for 15-18 minutes, stirring occasionally, until the rice is swollen and soft. Stir in the sugar to taste and let cool for 10 minutes.

3 Remove the vanilla bean from the rice, then stir in the yogurt. Serve sprinkled with a little nutmeg.

1 vanilla bean, halved lengthwise
1 cup short-grain rice
3 cups milk
2 tablespoons golden raisins
finely grated zest of 2 lemons
2 teaspoons granulated sugar, or to taste
2/3 cup thick plain yogurt
ground or freshly grated nutmeg, to serve

Serves **8**
Prep time **10 minutes, plus cooling**
Cooking time **20 minutes**

AFFORDABILITY 1

Warm Chocolate DESSERTS

1 Melt the chocolate in a heatproof bowl set over a saucepan of barely simmering water (do not let the bottom of the bowl touch the water), then remove from the heat. Add the fromage frais and vanilla extract and quickly stir together.

2 Divide the chocolate mixture among 6 little cups or glasses and serve immediately.

VARIATION

For warm cappuccino desserts, melt the semisweet chocolate with 2 tablespoons strong (brewed) espresso coffee and then add the fat-free fromage blanc, quark, or plain Greek yogurt. Divide among 6 espresso cups, finishing each with 1 teaspoon fromage blanc and a dusting of unsweetened cocoa powder.

10 oz semisweet chocolate, broken into squares
2 cups low-fat fromage blanc, quark, or plain Greek yogurt
1 teaspoon vanilla extract

Serves **6**
Prep time **5 minutes**
Cooking time **5 minutes**

WHITE *Chocolate* MOUSSE Ⓥ

1. Put the chocolate and milk into a heatproof bowl and melt over a saucepan of barely simmering water, making sure the bottom of the bowl does not touch the water.

2. To release the cardamom seeds, crush the pods using a mortar and pestle. Discard the pods and crush the seeds finely. Place the crushed cardamom seeds and the tofu in a blender or food processor with half of the sugar, then blend well to make a smooth paste. Turn the mixture into a large bowl.

3. Whisk the egg white in a separate clean bowl until it forms soft peaks. Gradually whisk in the remaining sugar.

4. Beat the melted chocolate mixture into the tofu until completely combined. Using a large metal spoon, fold in the whisked egg white.

5. Spoon the mousse into small coffee cups or glasses and chill in the refrigerator for at least 1 hour before serving. Serve topped with spoonfuls of crème fraîche or yogurt and a light dusting of unsweetened cocoa powder.

VARIATION
For white chocolate and amaretto cups, make the mousse mixture as above, omitting the cardamom and adding 2 tablespoons Amaretto liqueur when blending the tofu. Complete the recipe and chill as above. Serve with fresh raspberries instead of the crème fraîche or yogurt and cocoa powder.

7 oz white chocolate, chopped
¼ cup milk
12 cardamom pods
7 oz silken tofu
¼ cup granulated sugar
1 egg white
reduced-fat crème fraîche or plain Greek yogurt, to serve
unsweetened cocoa powder, for dusting

Serves **6-8**
Prep time **15 minutes, plus chilling**
Cooking time **5 minutes**

AFFORDABILITY 2

Apple Gelatin cups

1 Put the apples, cider, 2/3 cup water, sugar, and the zest of 1 of the lemons into a saucepan. Cover and simmer for 15 minutes, until the apples are soft.

2 Meanwhile, put the remaining 1/4 cup of water into a small bowl and sprinkle the gelatin over it, making sure that all the powder is absorbed by the water. Set aside.

3 Add the gelatin to the hot apples and stir until completely dissolved. Puree the apple mixture in a blender or food processor until smooth, then pour into 6 teacups or glasses. Let cool, then chill in the refrigerator for 4-5 hours, until completely set.

4 When you are ready to serve, whip the cream in a bowl until it forms soft peaks. Spoon the cream over the gelatins and sprinkle with the remaining lemon zest, then serve.

VARIATION
For apple cider granita, omit the gelatin and pour the pureed apple mixture into a shallow dish so that the mixture is about 1 inch deep or less. Freeze for about 2 hours, until mushy around the edges, then beat with a fork. Freeze for another 2 hours, beating the granita at 30-minute intervals, until it becomes the texture of crushed ice. Freeze until ready to serve, then scoop into small glasses.

6 cooking apples (about 2 lb), such as Granny Smiths, peeled, cored, and sliced
1¼ cups apple cider
2/3 cup water, plus 1/4 cup
1/3 cup granulated sugar
finely grated zest of 2 lemons
4 teaspoons powdered gelatin
2/3 cup heavy cream

Serves **6**
Prep time **20 minutes, plus cooling and chilling**
Cooking time **15 minutes**

Grilled Bananas
WITH BLUEBERRIES

1 Heat a ridged grill pan over medium-high heat, add the bananas, and grill for 8-10 minutes or until the skins are beginning to blacken, turning occasionally.

2 Transfer the bananas to serving dishes and, using a sharp knife, cut open lengthwise. Spoon the yogurt over the bananas and sprinkle with the oats and blueberries. Serve immediately, drizzled with about 1 teaspoon honey per banana.

VARIATION
For oat, ginger, and golden raisin yogurt, mix 1/2 teaspoon ground ginger with the yogurt in a bowl. Sprinkle with 2-4 tablespoons packed dark brown sugar, according to taste, the oats, and 1/4 cup golden raisins. Let stand for 5 minutes before serving.

4 bananas, unpeeled
1/2 cup nonfat Greek yogurt
1/4 cup rolled oats
1 cup blueberries
honey, to serve

Serves **4**
Prep time **5 minutes**
Cooking time **8-10 minutes,
plus standing**

Back to Basics

CHICKEN BROTH

PERFECT ROAST POTATOES

VEGETABLE BROTH

FRESH TOMATO SAUCE

PESTO

Vegetable Broth

THE VEGETABLES CAN VARY BUT MAKE SURE YOU INCLUDE SOME ONION AND OMIT VEGETABLES WITH STRONG FLAVORS AS WELL AS STARCHY ONES, SUCH AS POTATOES. FOR A DARK BROTH, LEAVE THE SKINS ON THE ONIONS AND USE PLENTY OF MUSHROOMS.

1 Heat the oil in a large, heavy saucepan and gently sauté all the vegetables for 5 minutes.

2 Add the water, bouquet garni, and peppercorns, bring slowly to a boil. Reduce the heat and simmer the broth gently for 40 minutes, skimming the surface from time to time, if necessary.

3 Strain the broth through a large strainer, preferably a conical one. Don't squeeze the juice out of the vegetables or the broth will be cloudy. Let the broth cool completely, then chill.

1 tablespoon sunflower oil
2 onions, coarsely chopped
2 carrots, coarsely chopped
2 celery sticks, coarsely chopped
1 (1 lb) package of other prepared vegetables or 4 cups prepared fresh vegetables, such as parsnips, fennel, leeks, zucchini, mushrooms, and tomatoes
6½ cups water
1 bouquet garni
1 teaspoon black peppercorns

Makes about **4 cups**
Prep time **10 minutes**
Cooking time **45 minutes**

CHICKEN BROTH

IDEALLY, CHICKEN BROTH IS MADE USING A RAW CARCASS, BUT A COOKED CARCASS ALSO MAKES A WELL-FLAVORED BROTH, IF A LITTLE CLOUDY.

1 Put the chicken carcass, giblets, onion, celery, bouquet garni or bay leaves, and peppercorns into a large, heavy saucepan or Dutch oven with the water.

2 Bring slowly to a boil. Reduce the heat and simmer the broth gently for 1½ hours, skimming the surface from time to time, if necessary.

3 Strain the broth through a large strainer, preferably a conical one. Let the broth cool completely, then chill.

1 large chicken carcass, plus any scraps
giblets, except the liver, if available
1 onion, quartered
1 celery stick, coarsely chopped
1 bouquet garni or 3 bay leaves
1 teaspoon black peppercorns
7½ cups cold water

Makes about **4 cups**
Prep time **10 minutes**
Cooking time **1½ hours**

GRAVY

GOOD-QUALITY CUTS OF ROASTED MEAT OR POULTRY PROVIDE DELICIOUS FATS AND JUICES FOR A WELL-FLAVORED GRAVY. AFTER ROASTING, LIFT THE MEAT FROM THE PAN, COVER IT LOOSELY WITH ALUMINUM FOIL, AND MAKE THE GRAVY WHILE THE MEAT STANDS.

1 Tilt the flameproof roasting pan and skim off the fat from the surface with a large serving spoon until you are left with the pan juices and just a thin layer of fat.

2 Over medium heat on the stove, sprinkle the flour into the pan and stir with a wooden spoon, scraping up all the residue, particularly from around the edges of the pan.

3 Gradually pour the liquid into the pan, stirring well until the gravy is thick and glossy. Let the mixture simmer, then check the seasoning, adding a little salt and black pepper, if necessary.

pan juices from roasted meat
1 tablespoon all-purpose flour
(less for a thin gravy)
1¼–1¾ cups liquid, such as:
water drained from the
accompanying vegetables;
broth; half broth and half water;
or half wine and half water
salt and black pepper

Makes about **2½ cups**
Cooking time **5 minutes**

OMELET

1 Break the eggs into a bowl and beat lightly with a wire whisk. Whisk in the water and season well with salt and black pepper. Do not overbeat, because it will ruin the texture of the finished omelet.

2 Set a small skillet over gentle heat and, when it is hot, add the butter. Tip the pan so that the entire inner surface is coated with butter. When the butter is foaming, but not browned, pour in the beaten eggs.

3 Let cook for a few seconds, then, using a spatula, draw the mixture away from the edge of the pan into the center, letting the eggs run to the sides. Repeat the process twice again, by which time the eggs should have set. Cook for another 30 seconds, until the underside is golden and top still slightly runny and creamy.

4 Tilt the pan and, with the spatula, carefully turn the omelet onto a plate, folding it in half in the process.

2 eggs
1 tablespoon water
1 tablespoon butter
salt and black pepper

Serves **1**
Prep time **2 minutes**
Cooking time **3-4 minutes**

STUDENT TIP

Grow your own … cooking herbs that is! You don't need a big yard—or any outside space for that matter (a windowsill will do)—to grow some essential herbs. For the price of a few plastic containers and packets of seeds, you could have your own collection of basil, parsley, and mint, ready to add another level to boring soups and sauces. Herbs also freeze well and you can use directly from frozen—so no more waste.

HOW TO MAKE *Perfect* ROAST POTATOES

NO SUNDAY DINNER IS COMPLETE WITHOUT POTATOES, SO IF YOU'RE IN DOUBT ON HOW TO MAKE DELICIOUS ROAST POTATOES, LOOK NO FARTHER.

1 Peel and cut potatoes into even-size pieces. Parboil in a saucepan of lightly salted boiling water for 10 minutes, then drain well. Shake them after draining to coarsen up the edges slightly.

2 Heat a roasting pan containing lard (or a good glug of sunflower oil for vegetarians and vegans) in a preheated oven, at 425°F, for about 5 minutes or until the lard or oil is hot. Carefully place the potatoes in it, turning them over in the oil, and then lightly sprinkle with sea salt.

3 Roast on the top shelf in the oven for 40 minutes, turning every now and then, until golden and crispy. Serve.

potatoes
lard or sunflower oil
sea salt

Serves **4-6**
Prep time **5 minutes**
Cooking time **55 minutes**

BOILED RICE

1 Put the rice in a strainer and wash it under running warm water, rubbing the grains together between your hands to get rid of any excess starch.

2 Put the rice into a saucepan and add the broth. Set the pan on the smallest ring on the stove and bring it to a boil. Give it a quick stir, then reduce the heat to a simmer. Cover with a lid and let cook for 15 minutes, or according to the package directions.

3 Turn off the heat and let the rice steam with the lid on for another 20 minutes. Don't be tempted to lift the lid to check what's going on.

4 To serve, fluff up the grains of rice with a spoon or fork.

2 cups Thai jasmine or long-grain rice
4 cups Vegetable or Chicken Broth (see pages 244)

Serves **4**
Prep time **5 minutes**
Cooking time **20 minutes, plus 20 minutes standing**

PESTO Ⓥ

MAKING PESTO TRADITIONALLY, USING A MORTAR AND PESTLE, FILLS THE AIR WITH THE WONDERFUL FRAGRANCE OF CRUSHED BASIL LEAVES, BUT IS MORE TIME-CONSUMING THAN THE QUICK AND EASY FOOD PROCESSOR METHOD USED HERE. FRESHLY MADE PESTO HAS NUMEROUS USES, MOST COMMONLY AS A PASTA SAUCE, BUT ALSO TO FLAVOR SOUPS, STEWS, AND RISOTTOS.

1 Tear the basil into pieces and put it into a blender or food processor with the pine nuts, cheese, and garlic.

2 Process lightly until the nuts are broken into small pieces, scraping the mixture down from the sides of the bowl, if necessary.

3 Add the oil and a little salt and black pepper, then blend to form a thick paste. Stir into freshly cooked pasta or turn into a bowl, cover, and refrigerate. It can be kept, covered, for up to 5 days.

VARIATION
To make red pesto, chop 1 cup drained sun-dried tomatoes in oil into small pieces, then add to the food processor instead of the basil.

1¼ cups fresh basil, including stems
⅓ cup pine nuts
¾ cup grated Parmesan-style cheese
2 garlic cloves, chopped
½ cup olive oil
salt and black pepper

Serves **4**
Prep time **5 minutes**

FRESH TOMATO SAUCE

THE RICH, FRUITY FLAVOR OF THIS SAUCE IS ONE OF THE BEST AND MOST USEFUL IN PASTA DISHES. USE IT AS IT IS OR ADD OTHER INGREDIENTS, SUCH AS CAPERS, ANCHOVIES, COOKED PANCETTA, OR TORN BASIL.

1 Put the tomatoes into a heatproof bowl, cover with boiling water, and let stand for about 2 minutes or until the skins start to split. Pour away the water. Skin and coarsely chop the tomatoes.

2 Heat the oil in a large, heavy saucepan and gently sauté the onion for 5 minutes or until softened but not browned. Add the garlic and sauté for another 1 minute.

3 Add the tomatoes and cook, stirring frequently, for 20-25 minutes or until the sauce is thickened and pulpy.

4 Stir in the oregano and season to taste with salt and black pepper. If the sauce is tart, add a sprinkling of granulated sugar, if desired.

TIP
This is a good sauce to make in large quantities if you have a lot of tomatoes and can be frozen in small plastic freezer bags or plastic containers.

VARIATION
Canned tomatoes make a good alternative if the only fresh ones available don't look appetizing. Substitute two (14½ oz) cans of diced tomatoes and cook until pulpy.

8 ripe, full-flavored tomatoes
  (about 2 lb)
½ cup olive oil
1 onion, finely chopped
2 garlic cloves, crushed
2 tablespoons chopped oregano
sprinkling of granulated sugar
  (optional)
salt and black pepper

Makes **3 cups**
Prep time **15 minutes**
Cooking time **30 minutes**

BÉCHAMEL SAUCE (V)

THIS CREAMY WHITE SAUCE IS USED AS A TOPPING FOR LASAGNE AND OTHER BAKED PASTA DISHES. IF THERE'S ALREADY CREAM IN THE PASTA RECIPE, YOU CAN USE EXTRA MILK INSTEAD.

1 Melt the butter over medium heat in a small, heavy saucepan. Stir in the flour and cook gently for 1-2 minutes, stirring to make a smooth paste.

2 Remove the pan from the heat and add the milk gradually (to avoid forming lumps) while continuously whisking or beating well with a wooden spoon. When all the milk is combined, you should have a smooth sauce.

3 Stir in the cream or additional milk, a little nutmeg, and salt and black pepper, then return the pan to the heat. Cook gently, stirring well, for about 2 minutes, until the sauce is smooth and thickened. Serve.

4 tablespoons butter
1/3 cup all-purpose flour
1¼ cups milk
1¼ cups light cream, or use
 2½ cups milk in total and
 omit the cream
freshly grated nutmeg, to taste
salt and black pepper

Makes **2½ cups**
Prep time **5 minutes**
Cooking time **10 minute**

PARSLEY SAUCE

THIS IS GREAT SERVED WITH FISH OR HAM.

1 Discard any tough stems from the parsley and put it into a blender or food processor or blender with half of the broth. Blend until the parsley is finely chopped.

2 Melt the butter over medium heat in a heavy saucepan until simmering. Add the flour and stir quickly to combine. Cook the mixture gently, stirring constantly with a wooden spoon, for 2 minutes.

3 Remove the pan from the heat and gradually whisk in the parsley-flavored broth, then the remaining broth, until smooth. Whisk in the milk. Return to the heat and bring to a boil, stirring. Season with salt and black pepper. Reduce the heat and continue to cook the sauce for about 5 minutes, stirring frequently, until it is smooth and glossy. The sauce should thinly coat the back of the spoon.

¼ cup parsley (choose really fresh, fragrant parsley)
1 cup Vegetable Broth (see page 244), fish broth, or ham broth
2 tablespoons butter
3 tablespoons all-purpose flour
1 cup milk
3 tablespoons light cream
salt and black pepper

Makes **2½ cups**
Prep time **10 minutes**
Cooking time **10 minute**

RED FRUIT COULIS

♡ *Vegan*

TWO OR THREE SUMMER FRUITS, BLENDED AND STRAINED TO PRODUCE A SMOOTH AND COLORFUL PUREE, MAKES A USEFUL SAUCE FOR SETTING OFF ALL KINDS OF DESSERTS. USE THE COULIS TO FLOOD THE SERVING PLATES OR DRIZZLE IT AROUND THE EDGES. EITHER WAY, IT WILL REALLY ENHANCE THE PRESENTATION. THIS COULIS IS GREAT SERVED WITH CHOCOLATE CHEESECAKE, VANILLA ICE CREAM, PANCAKES, AND FRUIT TARTS OR SIMPLY DRIZZLED OVER GREEK YOGURT.

1 Put the sugar into a liquid measuring cup and make it up to ¼ cup with boiling water. Stir until the sugar dissolves and then let cool.

2 Put all the fruits into a blender or food processor and blend to a smooth puree, scraping the mixture down from the sides of the bowl, if necessary. Blend in the sugar syrup.

3 Pour the sauce into a strainer set over a bowl. Press the puree with the back of a large metal spoon to squeeze out all the juice.

4 Stir in enough lemon juice to make the sauce slightly tangy, then transfer it to a small bowl. To serve, pour a little coulis onto each serving plate and gently tilt the plate so it is covered in an even layer. Alternatively, use a tablespoon to drizzle the sauce in a ribbon around the edges.

VARIATION
Replace up to 2 cups of the red fruits with fresh blueberries, blackberries, or berries and add 2–3 tablespoons crème de cassis or an orange liqueur. To make a more autumnal coulis, which is delicious with apple and banana desserts, use only blackberries and double the sugar.

3 tablespoons granulated sugar
about ¼ cup boiling water
4 cups fresh ripe red fruits, such as raspberries and hulled strawberries
2–3 teaspoons lemon juice

Serves **6-8**
Prep time **10 minutes, plus cooling**

AFFORDABILITY 2

INDEX

ACKNOWLEDGMENTS

Picture Credits
Dreamstime.com Absente 172 right; Al1962 243 below left; Artofphoto 136 above; Dušan Zidar 243 below right; Mallivan 75 above; Nataliya Arzamasova 173; Pojoslaw 227 left; Sanse293 75 below; Ukrphoto 172 left; Voyagerix 7; Wavebreakmedia Ltd 227 right; Zigzagmtart 243 above right. **istockphoto. com** damircudic 226; FangXiaNuo 136 below; joannawnuk 242; laflor 137 above; Leonardo Patrizi 137 below; monkeybusinessimages 205 right. **Octopus Publishing Group** Craig Robertson 26; David Munns 216 left, 229, 237; Emma Neish 35, 223; Gareth Sambidge 14, 15; Ian Wallace 37, 84, 113, 143, 203; Jason Lowe 133; Lis Parsons 2, 10, 18, 19, 27, 28, 31, 32, 39, 62, 73, 85, 86, 90, 94, 97, 98, 102, 104, 107, 108, 111, 121 below right, 122, 127, 146 below right, 146 above, 159, 165, 167, 169, 175, 179, 186 above right, 189, 209, 216 right, 217 left, 217 right, 218, 220, 221, 222, 232, 233, 235, 236; Sean Myers 191; Stephen Conroy 3 left, 33, 58, 59, 60, 61, 65, 69, 75 centre, 83, 100, 101, 106, 121 below left, 123, 130, 135, 139, 141, 166, 168, 186 above left, 190, 193, 206, 214, 248; Will Heap 3 right, 9, 17, 47, 49, 57, 72, 78, 79, 81, 89, 110, 146 below left, 151, 152, 153, 154, 157, 176, 178, 180, 186 below left, 195, 215, 234; William Lingwood 155, 163; William Reavell 8 left, 34, 40, 41, 43, 76, 121 above right, 132, 147, 181, 192, 194; William Shaw 8 right, 12, 20, 25, 29, 52, 54, 55, 63, 87, 93, 109, 121 above left, 134, 145, 161, 186 below right, 188, 199, 200, 205 left, 213, 224, 239, 240. **Shutterstock** AS Food studio 243 above left; cluckva 20 background; Curioso 4; designelements 60 background; Gencho Petkov 24-25; photastic 12-13; The_Pixel 10-11; vetkit 2-3. **Thinkstock** Hemera Technologies 29 background; Milos Luzanin 35 background.

Publisher Sarah Ford
Editor Pollyanna Poulter
Designers Eoghan O'Brien and Jaz Bahra
Picture Library Manager Jennifer Veall
Assistant Production Controller Meskerem Berhane

Extra recipes by Joanna Farrow
Features writer Cara Frost-Sharratt